Backpack to Briefcase

A Student's Guide to a
Meaningful Career Journey

By Stephanie Koonar
MBA, BA Psychology

PeerSpectives
consulting

Publisher's Cataloging-In-Publication Data

(Prepared by The Donohue Group, Inc.)

Names: Koonar, Stephanie, author.

Title: Backpack to briefcase : a student's guide to a meaningful career journey / by Stephanie Koonar, MBA, BA Psychology.

Description: 1st ed. | [Vancouver, British Columbia] : PeerSpectives Consulting, [2021] | Includes bibliographical references.

Identifiers: ISBN 9781777768607

Subjects: LCSH: Vocational guidance. | Job hunting. | Employment interviewing.

Classification: LCC HF5381 .K66 2021 | DDC 650.14083--dc23

PeerSpectives Consulting Company Inc.   www.PeerSpectives.ca
The author can be reached as follows: Stephanie@BackpacktoBriefcase.ca

Designed by Angie Ishak

Backpack to Briefcase, A Student's Guide to a Meaningful Career Journey, Stephanie Koonar.
--1st ed.

ISBN: 978-1-7777686-0-7

Table of Contents

cont'd

Exercises and Action Steps

PHASE 1: DISCOVER

cont'd

PHASE 2: BUILD

PHASE 3: LAUNCH

Introduction

We have all been there! You are out with your friends or family and you are asked that dreaded question:

"What are you going to do when you graduate?"

Your mind goes blank, your mouth goes dry—if only you had an answer.

If you haven't figured this out yet and you feel lost, confused, and not sure what the next steps are, then this book was written for you. Whether you are a high school student, a student in post-secondary education, or a recent graduate from a post-secondary institution, the steps in this book will help you chart your meaningful career journey.

A Bit About Me

I am Stephanie Koonar, I began my career in marketing. I worked in many different marketing roles in telecommunications, wine and spirit marketing, market research, and event marketing.

I then transitioned to teach marketing at the college level in the year 2000. I am an award-winning post-secondary instructor, and I have taught more than 4,000 students over the past 20 years. I have a Bachelor's degree in Psychology and a Master's degree in Business Administration. Currently I focus on career coaching.

Specifically, I work with students, facilitating their transition from student to career. But not transitioning to just any job but to roles that provide meaning and personal satisfaction. Roles that sometimes are the first of many steps along a meaningful career journey.

Finding and Living a Meaningful Career Journey

What does a meaningful career journey look like? Think about your career journey as an iterative process instead of a straight line. Your career journey is one that is built over your life and might be comprised of working in many different roles and jobs over time.

When you are on a meaningful career journey, you approach your work with anticipation, ready to use your natural strengths and abilities to make a difference. You are on a career path where you feel fulfilled, knowing that you are growing and thriving. You are happy and have peace of mind. In addition, you are financially independent—you have moved out of your family home and have started your adult life. Perhaps you have rented an apartment of your own. You feel confident, accomplished, and positive. You have both emotional and financial security.

A recent worldwide study conducted by Ipsos found that out of almost 20,000 adults surveyed, 48% indicated that one of the greatest sources of their happiness was "feeling that my life has meaning".[1] While on a meaningful career journey, you are living a life with purpose, knowing that you are making a positive impact on the world around you. Your journey energizes you as you move and pivot from role to role in response to growing and learning about yourself. You are content, and this comes from more than just fleeting moments of happiness, but rather a deep sense of meaning and purpose.

As a Gallup-Certified Strengths Coach, I was inspired to co-found a consulting firm based on coaching people to play to their strengths. My role allows me to coach individuals to be their best selves. I guest-speak at conferences and facilitate interactive workshops in-person and virtually. I am in a career that I love, that plays to my strengths, and I am energized every day by the positive impact I have.

But I was once in your shoes.

My "Aha!" Moment

After graduating high school in Ontario, I wasn't sure which career I wanted to pursue. My dad, however, wanted me to be a doctor. He worked at a medical publishing company. "I will get a great discount on the textbooks," he would say as a justification.

I had done well in science and math in high school, so I applied for the Natural Science program to complete a Bachelor of Science degree at McMaster University in Hamilton, Ontario. I was accepted into the program and enrolled in courses such as calculus, biology, physics, English, chemistry, and psychology.

However, by the end of my first term, I was failing calculus and physics, badly. I realized these were not the subjects that I wanted to continue studying. These were subjects that my dad wanted me to study to pursue a career that I was not excited about. In fact, I think my dad secretly wished that *he* had studied to become a doctor! I had to decide what I wanted to do. The path that I was on did not "feel right" to me.

However, there was a silver lining. During that first semester at university, I discovered one course I was enjoying and doing quite well in—psychology. By second semester, I decided to drop physics and I switched to a Bachelor of Arts degree in Psychology.

During my second year at university, I enrolled in subjects that were far more interesting to me and that I was excited to study. I took on a manageable workload and I enjoyed my studies.

Overall, it was a better fit for me. At the end of that year, I had made it onto the Dean's Honour List. I had redeemed myself and I felt that I was finding my way.

However—and I remember this next moment vividly—I was in my third year at university and studying in the library when a friend casually asked me, "What are you going to do when you graduate?"

Huh? What do you mean? This program doesn't lead anywhere? I realized that I had no idea what I was going to do after graduation. I did not have a plan. I hadn't thought about where this educational path was leading me. I hadn't started with an end in mind.

I didn't know I could take intentional steps towards uncovering a career that would be meaningful for me.

I have written this book because many people enroll in educational programs without really knowing if they will lead to a career that would be a good fit for them. They haven't taken the time to really understand themselves or know the job market. As a result, they spend unnecessary time and dollars trying to find their way. While this might work out in the long run for some people, I now know that there are proven steps that can guide you.

This book takes you through those proven steps. Steps that will save you valuable time and money. The chapters in this book have questions for you to answer to help you prepare for and discover what a truly meaningful career for you would look like. I will share plenty of stories about young adults just like you that took these steps and were able to successfully begin their meaningful career journey.

Let's get started!

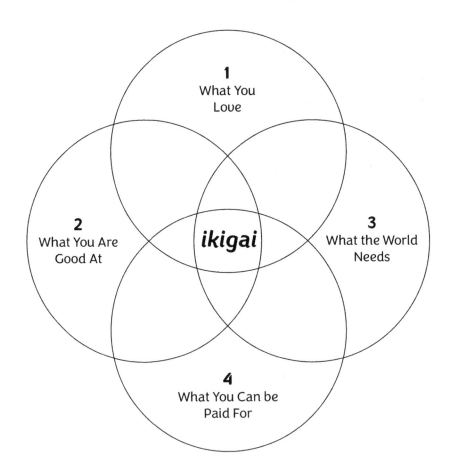

The *ikigai*

At this point, your path forward might be confusing. Perhaps you have decided on a career but you are not sure how to get there. Or maybe you have too many choices to consider and haven't been able to narrow it down. Or maybe you are in a post-secondary program and it just doesn't feel like a good fit.

We all have had this lack of clarity. Of not being sure what to do or if we are on the right path. It is difficult to really understand what different careers are all about if you haven't had a lot of experience.

So how do you move forward? I admit, this will require some work. The key is to start with understanding **you**. And hey, that is a subject you know something about!

When you take time to reflect, you can unlock a lot of understanding about yourself. You identify the ways you naturally think, act, and behave. Consider the interests and hobbies you love and what you truly value. You can discover your natural strengths and talents and recognize the unique gifts you offer to make the world better.

I call this the Discover Phase. By answering some key questions and conducting some research you will be able to narrow down your choices, charting out a path that you will feel excited about. As you navigate your career journey this way, see it as an adventure in learning, growing, and developing your inner sense of direction.

The Discover Phase includes reflecting on questions such as: What are you good at? What are your interests? What subjects do you like? But before we start the Discover Phase, I would like to introduce you to the idea of uncovering your *ikigai*.

Using the *ikigai* to Guide Your Path

Ikigai is a Japanese word that comes from "iki" meaning life and "kai" meaning the realization of hopes and expectations.[2] The meaning of the two words together is roughly: a reason for being or a sense of purpose and is pronounced "*ee-key-guy*".

Discovering your *ikigai* comes from answering the questions in each of the four circles in the *ikigai* diagram. Where these four circles intersect, you will find your *ikigai*, or your true purpose.

Your *ikigai* diagram is a useful reference to check in with as you navigate your meaningful career journey. You can modify, add to, and adapt your *ikigai* diagram. It's constantly evolving as you learn and grow.

ikigai Diagram

Where the four circles intersect is the sweet spot—your *ikigai*! Imagine if you could find a career that allows you to bring together what you love, what you are good at, what the world needs and what you can be paid for!

In this book, this model will guide you to discover meaningful career opportunities. I will provide you with steps to take, questions to answer, and activities to complete that will reveal information to add to your own *ikigai* diagram. There are blank *ikigai* diagram pages found at the back of this book to write your answers in. The next four chapters will walk you through ways to reflect on each of the *ikigai* circles. Let me review the *ikigai* diagram in more detail:

Circle One is labelled "What You Love" and refers to your interests, passions, and the values that you hold close.

Circle Two is labelled "What You Are Good At" and refers to your natural talents, skills, and knowledge.

Circle Three is labelled "What the World Needs" and requires you to think about your most important concerns about the world and how your unique strengths and qualities might play a role in solving them.

Circle Four is labelled "What You Can be Paid For" and refers to identifying the type of jobs that will be in demand in the future and if they will be well-paid jobs.

Your Goal: Intersecting the Four Circles

To achieve a meaningful career, having all four circles intersect is optimal. While there are numerous variations of overlapping two or three of these circles, let's see how missing one or more circles will leave you wanting.

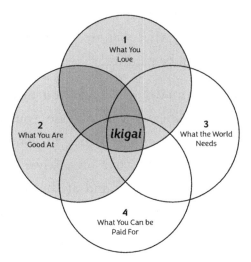

This work is a derivative of Ikigai-EN.svg by Nimbosa, an adaptation from works in the PUBLIC DOMAIN by Dennis Bodor (SVG) and Emmy van Deurzen (JPG), CC BY-SA 4.0 <https://creativecommons.org/licenses/by-sa/4.0>, via Wikimedia Commons/ Some words removed from the original.

Intersecting "What You Love" with "What You Are Good At"

Imagine if just two of the circles were intersecting: circle one, "What You Love" and circle two, "What You Are Good At". This might mean you spend your time doing an activity that is in synch with your passion AND you are good at it—and it's great that you have a passion! Your passion might be playing a musical instrument, making pottery, hiking, or running. I think it is wonderful to reflect on your passions and interests and see what elements really bring you joy.

The great news is that it is quite possible to turn your passion into a role that you can get paid for if there is a demand for it: if you became a paid musician or you sold your pottery, or perhaps you were paid to lead hiking trips or held running clinics where you are financially compensated.

However, if there isn't a large enough demand for what you are offering, then while you may be following your passion and be good at it, you might not be able to have financial independence through your passion alone. Part of the Discover Phase is confirming that your future career choices will be in demand and will pay you well, hence why circle four, "What You Can be Paid For" needs to be included.

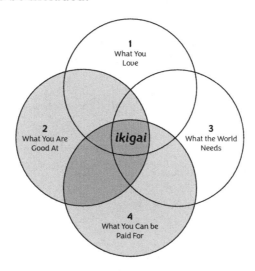

This work is a derivative of Ikigai-EN.svg by Nimbosa, an adaptation from works in the PUBLIC DOMAIN by Dennis Bodor (SVG) and Emmy van Deurzen (JPG), CC BY-SA 4.0 <https://creativecommons.org/licenses/by-sa/4.0>, via Wikimedia Commons/ Some words removed from the original.

Intersecting "What You Are Good At" with "What You Can be Paid For"

Now, what if the only two circles that were intersecting were circle two and circle four? Circle two, "What You Are Good At" refers to your talents, skills, and knowledge. Circle four is called "What You Can be Paid For" and refers to a role that can support your financial independence. If these two circles were intersecting, this could mean that you do have the skills and knowledge for your job so you are good at it (circle two). Plus, you are getting paid well (circle four). This sounds pretty good, doesn't it? However, what is missing? You might find over time that this situation is not in line with your passion and values (circle one) or that it doesn't provide you with a sense of meaning (circle three). As a result, you may experience dissatisfaction and have a feeling of being unfulfilled sometime along the way.

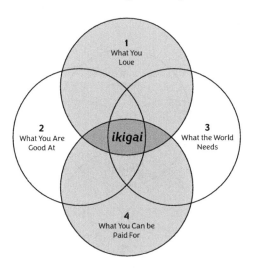

This work is a derivative of Ikigai-EN.svg by Nimbosa, an adaptation from works in the PUBLIC DOMAIN by Dennis Bodor (SVG) and Emmy van Deurzen (JPG), CC BY-SA 4.0 <https://creativecommons.org/licenses/by-sa/4.0>, via Wikimedia Commons/ Some words removed from the original.

Intersecting "What You Love" with "What You Can be Paid For"

Continuing on, what if you do find a role that you are passionate about (circle one), AND you are paid well for it (circle four) but you do NOT have the knowledge or skills to do the job (circle two)? That just means you need to set a plan to acquire the skills, knowledge, and education that is required, so that you can get good at it!

So the key to having a truly meaningful career is finding a career that meets all four criteria. Circle three, "What the World Needs", asks you to identify the issues in the world that need solving and speak directly to you. What issue drives you crazy that no one seems to care about? Are there conditions in the world that you want to fix or improve? You can use your talents and strengths to help solve the challenges that you have identified, pointing you in a direction towards a very meaningful career.

A meaningful career is one that allows you to do what you love, do what you are good at, be well-paid to do it, and solves or addresses something that the world needs!

While in the Discover Phase, I will show you the steps to filling out your own *ikigai* diagram. Students, executives, managers, graduates, and alumni have all taken these steps to answer key questions as part of their discovery. Clients I have coached have found this exploration very illuminating in helping them chart their futures. Throughout this book, I provide questions and activities for you to reflect on and there is space to write your answers throughout.

Or if you prefer, scan this QR code to download a free fillable PDF workbook and find other resources such as coaching and information on the online courses.

You can also go to: www.backpacktobriefcase.ca/workbook.

PHASE 1
DISCOVER

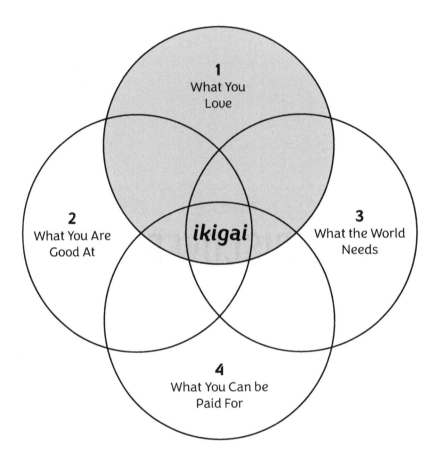

CHAPTER 1

What You Love

In the next few chapters, I will provide you with the steps to take and questions to answer for filling out your *ikigai* diagram at the back of this book. Let's start with the first circle of the *ikigai* diagram, called "What You Love" and delve into the related area of what you value. These are the first two steps in filling out circle one on your *ikigai* diagram.

Have you thought about what you really love? The types of things you are drawn to that give you energy and excite you? Or are you not quite sure what those things are?

Step 1: Look to Your Hobbies and Interests for What You Love

One way to identify what you love is to examine your hobbies and interests. Listing the activities that you participate in during your spare time is a great place to start. For example, do you love painting? Are you into reading about medieval history? Are you musically inclined? Or maybe you're mechanically inclined—someone that loves breaking down and rebuilding engines or small machines.

Let's begin with some questions to uncover what you love:

1. List the interests, hobbies, and extracurricular activities that you have enjoyed participating in over the past few years.

_____

_____

2. List the school subjects you like and tend to do well in.

_____

_____

3. Consider the YouTube videos that you subscribe to or the influencers that you follow. List them here.

_____

_____

4. How about books? When you go into a bookstore, which section of the bookstore do you tend to visit?

_____

How can a hobby provide ideas about a career? Can you have a career doing something you love? Well, let me share Audrey's story with you.

Audrey's Success Story:
From Accountant to Interior Decorator

Audrey was an accountant by day, but her real passion was home design and décor. In her spare time, she worked on all types of decorating projects. She would repaint her bedroom every year, or redecorate her living room, or help friends re-arrange their living room furniture. Audrey would spend endless hours in a paint store, just looking at paint colour chips and wall-paper books.

Audrey wanted to add to her decorating knowledge and decided to take a certificate at a local college on home decorating while still working in her accounting role. Then slowly, on a part-time basis, she launched her OWN home design business, adding clients one by one. Eventually, her company was making enough money that she was able to leave her role as an accountant. She successfully ran her décor business on a full-time basis for 15 years. Her clients included subdivision builders, individuals, and condominium developers.

What to do if you don't know what you love? Did your reflections on the previous questions leave you thinking you might not have any interests you're really passionate about? My advice is to keep exploring and be open to new opportunities. This is a journey! Take a course, enroll in further study or volunteer to find out what fits. It is okay to start down a path just to learn and collect data about yourself. Many students while in college or university find out about themselves by taking different subjects. It is perfectly normal to see students switch their focus of their studies based on this information. This happened to me when I was at university as I previously shared.

Step 2: What Do You Value?

Your values shape who you are. Your values influence your decisions. Your values are often instinctual and as a result, you may not be able to easily identify your values. One way to uncover what you really value is to review a list of value words and see which words you connect with. These also might be qualities that you want to see more of in the world.

From the list, circle the value words that you connect with, words that are important to you. Consider that these are qualities that you want to see more of the world. Feel free to add a value word if you feel it should be on the list!

Value Words

appreciation	inclusiveness
authenticity	kindness
boldness	optimism
cheerfulness	originality
collaboration	passion
compassion	perseverance
courage	playfulness
creativity	professionalism
curiosity	resilience
determination	resourcefulness
diversity	responsibility
empathy	self-confidence
enthusiasm	self-discipline
excellence	self-expression
fairness	sense-of-beauty
generosity	sense-of-belonging
gratitude	sense-of-community
growth	spirit-of-adventure
happiness	sportsmanship
health	teamwork
honesty	thoughtfulness
humility	wisdom
humour	

Select no more than 10 of the value words you circled from the list. Knowing these values and keeping them in mind will provide you with a way to evaluate if an organization or a future employer share and value the same things that you do. Write them down below.

1.	
2.	
3.	
4.	
5.	
6.	
7.	
8.	
9.	
10.	

Summary

Noting and reflecting on the things that you are interested in and what you value, provides you with important information that could lead you to a career that will be fulfilling and exciting to you.

Amelia, a student that participated in one of our career workshops, sent me a lovely thank you card stating:

> *"I previously felt as if I had to pursue a career in my strongest academic subject areas but I am now thinking about how I could incorporate my extracurricular interests into a more enjoyable and fulfilling career path."*

Identifying your value words uncovers what you truly value allowing you to add those words to your *ikigai* diagram in circle one, "What You Love" at the back of the book.

In Chapter 2, I will pose questions for you to reflect on and answer to uncover what you are uniquely good at so you can add these insights to the "What You Are Good At" (circle two) in your *ikigai* diagram.

Checklist

☐ Identify what you love!

    ☐ List the interests, hobbies, and extracurricular activities that you have enjoyed participating in over the past few years

    ☐ List the school subjects you like and tend to do well in

    ☐ Consider the YouTube videos that you stream or the influencers that you follow

    ☐ When you visit a bookstore, name the section of the bookstore you tend to visit

    ☐ Add what you love to circle one of your *ikigai* diagram

☐ Identify your 10 value words

    ☐ Add your value words to circle one of your *ikigai* diagram at the back of the book

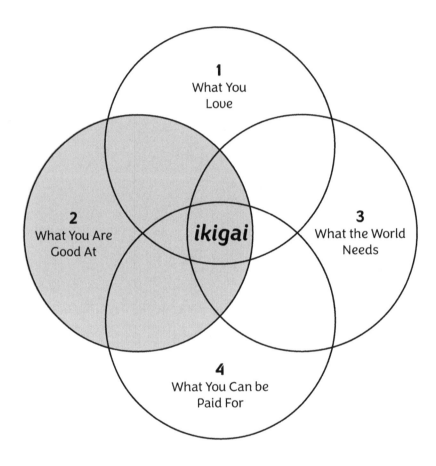

CHAPTER 2

What You Are Good At

In the last chapter, you identified what you love and value. The next area to explore so that you can add to your *ikigai* diagram is circle two, "What You Are Good At".

One way to uncover what you are good at or what you naturally do well is to reflect on past accomplishments that you are proud of. These accomplishments might have happened at school, while you were volunteering, or when you were at work. Coming up with an example may take you some time but that is all right. Write down a description of your accomplishment. Then look at the situation closely, analyze it, and break down the steps you took to achieve it. By doing this exercise, you will isolate how you tend to tackle projects. The way you tackle projects is unique to you, as unique as how you think, act, and behave. When you are working on something that you enjoy doing, you tend to lean into your strengths or natural qualities to accomplish it. We tend to solve problems or address opportunities using our special talents and natural capabilities.

Let's begin uncovering what you're good at by answering the following questions:

Step 3: Reflect On a Past Accomplishment

Recall a situation when you accomplished something you were proud of. It could have happened at school, work, while volunteering, or in the community. It was a time when your energy was high, you felt engaged, inspired, and you were in the "flow"! It was something you loved doing!

Write out a description of that situation.

_____

_____

_____

_____

_____

_____

Analyze the situation by breaking down the steps you used to accomplish this success. How did you tackle the project? What unique skills or strengths did you use? List them here.

_____

_____

_____

One way to understand what you are good at is to look for patterns in the skills used over a couple of accomplishments that you are proud of. Let's look at Hiroko and her accomplishments to see how to identify patterns. When asked about a time when she accomplished something she was proud of, Hiroko immediately mentions that she completed a 10 kilometre race.

When you ask her to outline the steps she used to make this accomplishment happen, she will tell you that she divided her training into daily and weekly numerical goals, and put herself on a training session schedule with her local run club. She analyzed her progress through tracking apps on her phone. Hiroko also researched nutritional websites, planning out her daily nutritional requirements for her monthly training schedule. These planning and organizing skills were skills that she loved to use and were skills she was good at.

Hiroko's Success Story:
Run a Race, Run an Event

On the day of the race she was very happy to successfully complete the event. And she realized that she enjoyed the planning of it, almost as much as completing the race itself.

When Hiroko was asked for another accomplishment that she was proud of, she said it was when she organized a fundraiser. She reflected on the steps that she took, noting that she first researched online to obtain quotes and then analyzed the data to select the right suppliers. She then scheduled out all the tasks to complete. These were things she liked to do and that came easy to her.

If we look for patterns in the steps that Hiroko took to be successful in both these situations, you can see that Hiroko tends to lean into her strengths or skills in:

- Planning, setting goals, and scheduling details (detail-oriented)

- Setting direction (directive)

- Analyzing and working with numbers (numerical ability)

- Researching websites and articles (written comprehension skills)

Skills such as planning and scheduling are very important skills for an event planning role and show that a person is detail-oriented. You'll notice I've categorized Hiroko's skills in the brackets, using words that employers would identify as "job skills" or "occupational skills".

Identifying these skills and strengths is particularly useful information. In fact, these are the types of skills that employers want to know about. Hiroko can highlight this understanding of her skills in interviews in the future.

Occupational Skills: Do You Have What It Takes?

Occupational skills are the knowledge, skills, and abilities needed for a certain occupation. Required occupational skills have been identified for a variety of jobs by the Provincial Government Department: Work BC. In fact, there are 147 career profiles you can review at www.careertrekbc.ca[3] that outline the occupational skills required for them. There are also video interviews of professionals working in their careers. A search for "event planner" on the website reveals a video of an interview with an event planner.

In the video, the event planner outlines the daily duties and the education required for this career.

The event planner profile on the website includes a list of the occupational skills required to be successful in this role. The role requires someone that is detail-oriented, directive, has numerical ability, and has verbal and written comprehension skills.

By looking for patterns in how Hiroko tackled completing a 10 kilometre run and managed the fundraising event you can see that she has some of the occupational skills that are required for a career in event planning. These examples will be useful when interviewing as she can comfortably share the occupational skills that she would bring to an event planner role based on her experience.

Your turn:

Step 4: Looking for Patterns

Reflect on two accomplishments from your past that you are proud of—one of the accomplishments can be from Step 3. The situations could be a volunteer opportunity or something great that you worked on at a job or at school.

Write out a brief description for each situation.

_____

_____

_____

_____

_____

_____

For each accomplishment, make a list of the steps you took to achieve your goals.

_____

_____

_____

Review your lists. Do you recognize any patterns? Are there skills you tended to use in both situations? Do you recognize the key skills that you are good at? List them here:

_____

_____

_____

Self-Assessment Tools

Another way to determine what you are good at is to use a self-assessment tool. An assessment or questionnaire can help you to identify your talents and your occupational skills. They can be fun to complete and the results are very informative, providing you with a starting place for career exploration! Career Cruising, Myers-Briggs®, 16 Personalities, and CliftonStrengths® are the ones I recommend for career-focused discovery.

Xello, formerly Career Cruising

Perhaps you have used Xello, formerly known as Career Cruising, at your school. Through the Xello platform you can complete a variety of assessments to help you better understand your unique interests, skills, and strengths. Students can explore hundreds of career options matching their skills. It's a great jumping off point for further career exploration, ask your school counselors if they offer the program.[4]

Myers-Briggs Type Indicator®

You might be familiar with the Myers-Briggs Type Indicator® assessment. This assessment asks you questions and then analyzes the results to indicate your personality preferences in four dimensions. On completion of the assessment you are assigned four letters, one from each box.

Where you focus your attention: Extraversion (**E**) or Introversion (**I**)	**How you make decisions:** Thinking (**T**) or Feeling (**F**)
The way you take in information: Sensing (**S**) or INtuition (**N**)	**How you deal with the world:** Judging (**J**) or Perceiving (**P**)

Source: The Myers-Briggs® Company
https://eu.themyersbriggs.com/en/tools/MBTI/MBTI-personality-Types accessed May 20, 2021

The Myers-Briggs® assessment has been offered since 1962, and it is estimated that 50 million people have taken the test. Usage in the United States, according to an article in the *Washington Post*, suggests that "somewhere around 10,000 companies, 2,500 colleges and universities, and 200 government agencies use the Myers-Briggs® test."[5]

There are many additional products, books, and coaching services available to support further understanding of your Myers-Briggs® type. One book that links type to career profiles is called *Do What You Are: Discover the Perfect Career for You Through the Secrets of Personality Type* by Paul D. Tieger, Barbara Barron, and Kelly Tieger and is available on Amazon. The book identifies different occupations that tend to be popular by type and provides workbook exercises to help readers with their job search.[6]

You might consider approaching your high school counsellor or post-secondary institution career centre to find out if the Myers-Briggs® assessment is available to students. This assessment must be delivered through a licensed administrator.

16Personalities

This assessment uses the same four-letter acronyms as some other frameworks, however, 16Personalities has added an extra letter to accommodate an additional scale[7] of either Assertive (A) or Turbulent (T) that reflects your confidence in your abilities and decisions.

16Personalities has four main roles; Analysts, Diplomats, Sentinels, and Explorers and within those roles, four additional types as follows:

Analysts: Architect, Logician, Commander, Debater

Diplomats: Advocate, Mediator, Protagonist, Campaigner

Sentinels: Logistician, Defender, Executive, Consul

Explorers: Virtuoso, Adventurer, Entrepreneur, Entertainer

Find out more at www.16personalities.com and also complete a free assessment.

Gallup CliftonStrengths®

Another online assessment tool is the CliftonStrengths® assessment. The assessment was developed by Don Clifton, PhD, a psychologist and business executive who was known to say, "What will happen when we think about what is right with people rather than fixating on what is wrong with them?"[8]

Dr. Clifton is responsible for developing CliftonStrengths® which is administered by GALLUP®, a data-driven management consulting business known for the Gallup Poll®. Over 25 million people have taken the assessment. Based on positive psychology, the CliftonStrengths® assessment is a tool used at many Fortune 500 companies including Southwest Airlines, Levi's Jeans, Facebook, and TELUS. Companies use the CliftonStrengths® assessment to help their employees identify their own strengths and to also learn and appreciate the strengths in their colleagues.

The assessment is provided to students on 600+ campuses in North America. Studies have shown that college students who participate in strength-based programs have improved self-confidence, direction, hope, and altruism.[9]

GALLUP® offers the Top 5 CliftonStrengths® online assessment for about $30 CAD. The assessment takes approximately 30 minutes to complete. You will receive two reports describing your Top 5 Strengths, outlining how you naturally think, behave and act.

As a Gallup-Certified Strengths Coach at PeerSpectives Consulting, I have used this assessment with hundreds of people to bring attention to their natural talents. This tool has allowed people to gain a better understanding and appreciation of the value they bring to the world and how to recognize the value that others bring. The Top 5 CliftonStrengths® report identifies your natural talents. You can refine and hone these talents into strengths with knowledge, skills, awareness, and practice.[10] According to GALLUP® people who have the opportunity to use their strengths at work are six times as likely to be engaged in their jobs and more than three times as likely to report having an excellent quality of life.[11]

You can get insight into identifying your strengths by reflecting on times when you seemed to learn how to do something quite quickly. Typically, you feel "in the flow of the moment" when you are using a strength. In those moments, people see glimpses of excellence in you. You feel a sense of satisfaction using your strengths and once finished, you want to do it again. In fact, you have a "yearning" to do it again.[12]

Step 5: Top Strengths or Qualities

If you have completed the CliftonStrengths® assessment, write down your Top 5 Strengths here, or if you like, think of five personal qualities that you have to offer the world and list those.

1. _____

2. _____

3. _____

4. _____

5. _____

It helps to be aware of your strengths and qualities. The CliftonStrengths® assessment gives you the vocabulary to name your natural talents and to acknowledge that your strengths have always been part of you, something that you might not have recognized before.

Jasmine's Experience with Her Strengths

Knowing your strengths allows you to know what you bring to a team. Sometimes it is hard to recognize what you naturally do as a strength. See if you can recognize the strength that Jasmine brings to a team:

Jasmine's Success Story:
Being Responsible

Jasmine is a very focussed student. She is the kind of student that is always aware of due dates. In a team project, she is the one that keeps the group on-task and often sets the timelines and deliverables. This is her strength and when she looks at her CliftonStrengths® report, she sees that her number one strength is Responsibility®. A person like Jasmine with the Responsibility® strength ensures that deadlines are met and ensures the group members all stay on track.

Knowing your strengths can help you identify roles that require what you are good at! This will lead to fulfilling roles that energize you. I know my strengths have been very helpful in understanding which roles I am attracted to and the roles where I can use my strengths.

My Own Experience With My Strengths

In my role as a marketing instructor, I use many of my strengths, or what I am good at, and this has contributed to satisfaction in my career. My Top 5 Strengths are Communication®, Woo®, Futuristic®, Maximizer®, and Positivity®.

As a marketing instructor, I teach marketing communications courses which allows me to use my verbal and written Communication® strength. I am also a promoter and champion of many initiatives at my place of work and that is where I direct my Woo® talent. "Woo" stands for "Winning Over Others" and is a strength that naturally seeks to meet people, cheerlead and enthusiastically champion ideas. In my role as Assistant Chair, External Relations, I sought out many external partners to connect students to, and provided them with work-integrated learning opportunities. That was one of the most enjoyable parts of my career and I leaned heavily into this talent. My strength of Positivity® shows up in the classroom, where I aim to bring laughter and a sense of fun to my teaching practice.

In a previous career as a marketing researcher, I leaned into my Futuristic® strength to seek out and read research reports, scanning reports for marketing trends. And I have used this strength in my role as Marketing Manager at TELUS, to plan out year-long advertising campaigns.

I am very energized when I help individuals and teams understand their strengths so they can improve, grow, and thrive, taking good to great! This is a key attribute of someone that has the Maximizer® strength.

Add Your Strengths to your *ikigai* Diagram

Now that you have identified what you are good at, go list your strengths and qualities in circle two "What You Are Good At" on your *ikigai* diagram at the back of the book.

Summary:

In this chapter, you were introduced to ways of discovering what you are good at. I included exercises for you to complete that will help you uncover key information about yourself.

I suggested the following assessments to identify your strengths and qualities:

- Xello, formerly Career Cruising
- Myers-Briggs® test
- 16Personalities
- CliftonStrengths®

Understanding what you are good at will help you chart your way along your meaningful career journey!

In the next chapter, we will look at questions that can help you fill out circle three called "What the World Needs". We will explore important issues the world is facing and how your unique strengths and qualities might play a role in solving them.

Checklist

Determining what you are good at:

☐ Reflect on your past accomplishments to spot your unique skills

☐ Look for patterns to pull out the skills that you use most frequently

Consider taking some suggested self-assessments such as:

☐ Xello, formerly Career Cruising

☐ Myers-Briggs®

☐ 16Personalities

☐ CliftonStrengths®

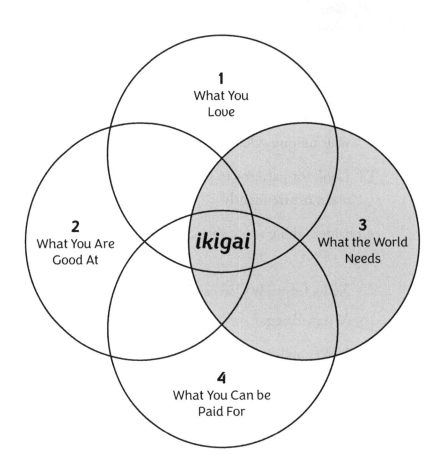

CHAPTER 3

What the World Needs

In the previous chapters, we looked at discovering what you love and what you are good at. If you recall, you identified your value words in Chapter 1. Knowing your value words will inform you as you delve into exploring "What the World Needs", circle three of the *ikigai* diagram.

In this chapter, we will investigate what the world needs and how that might guide you on your meaningful career journey.

If you are a student or a graduate who is looking to work for companies and organizations that align with your values, you are not alone. According to a Deloitte report, Gen Z (those born since 2000) looks beyond a company's products and seeks to understand an organization's ethics, practices, and social impact. This is wonderful![13]

Understanding a company's ethics is an important consideration when evaluating employers to work for. Research suggests that Gen Z is determined to make a difference and make an impact. One of those ways is through social entrepreneurship. In fact, "social entrepreneurship is one of the most popular career choices emerging."[14]

A social entrepreneur wishes to solve social, environmental, or cultural issues through funds generated by their business and have a transformational benefit for a segment of society.[15] A social enterprise could be a non-profit organization that engages in for-profit activities to generate income for their social mission. Or, as stated, a social enterprise might be a for-profit business that tries to solve community or environmental challenges and provides their employees meaningful work.[16]

Gavin, a former student, was able to find important work after he graduated at a social enterprise that aligned with his values.

Gavin's Success Story:
Using His Strengths to Strengthen Others

Gavin joined the Eastside Movement for Business and Economic Renewal Society (EMBERS) as the Director of Operations after graduating from his business program. He shared that, "This role provides me with meaning and satisfaction as I apply my strengths and talents to help people facing barriers to obtaining work. EMBERS offers employment opportunities including job placements, training and support and I loved it from day one!"[17]

It is worthwhile spending time reflecting on what is important to you and what cause or purpose you can aim your talents at. And it's actually good for you in the long run. The book entitled, *The Purposeful Graduate*, describes studies that show "purpose exploration has actual enduring and beneficial effects on graduates' overall life satisfaction."[18]

Will every job tie into your purpose? Not necessarily, but maybe. It depends on how you see it.

Job, Career, or Calling: What's the Difference?

Shawn Achor, in his book called, *The Happiness Advantage*, refers to the research of Yale psychologist Amy Wrzesniewski where she found that employees can have three "work orientations". We can see our work as a Job, Career, or Calling. If we see it as a Job, then our work is more of a chore and the pay is the reward. When people see their work as a Career, they see the opportunity to advance, succeed, and they want to do well. However, the people that see their work as a Calling, "view work as an end in itself; their work is fulfilling not because of external rewards but because they feel it contributes to the greater good, draws on their personal strengths, and gives them meaning and purpose."[19]

Research conducted by the Brainstorm Strategy Group with 16,0000 post-secondary students indicated that after "balancing work-life with personal life", students stated that their most important career goal is to "feel that I am serving a cause or greater good."[20]

So how do we start to uncover what is going to be a meaningful purpose for us? You have already identified your values. Next, it is time to reflect on what issues are important to you.

There are a lot of issues that the world is facing on this planet. The good news is that increased activism shows that people want to see changes in the world and are doing something about it. Each of us connects to different issues. You might be concerned for the environment and see that as the primary issue to address. Or you may wish to focus on reducing poverty in the world to bring about more equity. Or perhaps you wish to support single parents, or help abandoned animals, or tackle systemic issues to promote more justice, equity, diversity, and inclusion in your community.

The United Nations Sustainable Development Goals: Where Do you Fit In?

In case you haven't heard about them, I would like to introduce you to the United Nations Sustainable Development Goals (SDGs) aimed to be achieved by 2030. You can find out more at www.un.org/sustainabledevelopment.

Source: "Sustainable Development Goals, Guidelines for the use of the SDG LOGO, including the Colour Wheel and 17 icons," page 43, accessed May 18th, 2021 https://www.un.org/sustainabledevelopment/news/communications-material/

Many organizations and individuals are applying their talents in addressing these goals. And I love that Vicki Saunders, Founder of SheEO, calls these goals "the World's To-Do List".[21] The SheEO organization is a community supporting women and non-binary people working on these challenges. More information on the support this organization provides is found at www.sheeo.world.

We can hone in on the 17 SDGs that might be of interest to you by first considering the "5 P" categories as outlined in the *Sustainable Foundation, A Guide for Teaching the Sustainable Development Goals*, produced by the Manitoba Council for International Cooperation.[22] Review the categories and select the "P" that most resonates with you as outlined in Step 6.

Step 6: Review the 5 Ps and Check the Categories that are of Interest to You

People	We are determined to end poverty and hunger, in all their forms and dimensions, and to ensure that all human beings can fulfill their potential in dignity and equality and in a healthy environment.	
Planet	We are determined to protect the planet from degradation, including through sustainable consumption and production, sustainable management of natural resources and by taking urgent action on climate change, so that the planet can support the needs of present and future generations.	
Prosperity	We are determined to ensure that all human beings can enjoy prosperous and fulfilling lives and that economic, social, and technological progress occurs in harmony with nature.	
Peace	We are determined to foster peaceful, just, and inclusive societies, which are free from fear and violence. There can be no sustainable development without peace and no peace without sustainable development.	
Partnership	We are determined to implement this agenda through a global partnership, based on a spirit of global solidarity, focused in particular on the needs of the poorest and most vulnerable, and with the participation of all countries, all stakeholders and all people.	

Source: Data from "Sustainable Foundations: A Guide for Teaching the Sustainable Development Goals," Manitoba Council for International Cooperation, 2020, iii, accessed Jan 31st, 2021, http://mcic.ca/uploads/public/files-sf/SF-Full-FINAL-WEB-ISBN-2021-EN.pdf.

The 17 United Nations Sustainable Development Goals

Let's dive a little deeper to understand the 17 SDGs, reviewing the brief descriptions in the table. As you review each goal, select any that you are drawn to. Are there any goals that you wish to be a part of solving? Can you imagine working on solving these goals with others, dedicated to making a positive impact in the world? Do you see a pattern in the type of challenges you wish to tackle?

Step 7: Select the UN SDGs that Resonate With You

17 UN SDGs	✔
Goal 1: No Poverty: End poverty in all its forms, everywhere	
Goal 2: Zero Hunger: End hunger, achieve food security and improved nutrition and promote sustainable agriculture	
Goal 3: Good Health and Well-being: Ensure healthy lives and promote well-being for all at all ages	
Goal 4: Quality Education: Ensure inclusive and equitable quality education and promote lifelong learning opportunities for all	
Goal 5: Gender Equality: Achieve gender equality and empower all women and girls	
Goal 6: Clean Water and Sanitation: Ensure availability and sustainable management of water and sanitation for all	
Goal 7: Affordable and Clean Energy: Ensure access to affordable, reliable, sustainable and modern energy for all	
Goal 8: Decent Work and Economic Growth: Promote sustained, inclusive and sustainable economic growth, full and productive employment and decent work for all	

Goal 9: Industry, Innovation and Infrastructure: Build resilient infrastructure, promote inclusive and sustainable industrialization and foster innovation	
Goal 10: Reduced Inequalities: Reduce inequality within and among countries	
Goal 11: Sustainable Cities and Communities: Make cities and human settlements inclusive, safe, resilient and sustainable	
Goal 12: Responsible Consumption and Production: Ensure sustainable consumption and production patterns	
Goal 13: Climate Action: Take urgent action to combat climate change and its impacts	
Goal 14: Life Below Water: Conserve and sustainably use the oceans, seas and marine resources for sustainable development	
Goal 15: Life on Land: Protect, restore and promote sustainable use of terrestrial ecosystems, sustainably manage forests, combat desertification, and halt and reverse land degradation and halt biodiversity loss	
Goal 16: Peace, Justice and Strong Institutions: Promote peaceful and inclusive societies for sustainable development, provide access to justice for all and build effective, accountable and inclusive institutions at all levels	
Goal 17: Partnerships for the Goals: Strengthen the means of implementation and revitalize the global partnership for sustainable development	

Source: SDG Guide. "Getting Started with the SDGs" page 6, accessed May 18, 2021 https://resources.unsdsn. org/sdg-guide-getting-started-with-the-sdgs

You might wonder: What are the types of careers that tackle these challenges? One innovative way to uncover which careers are solving these issues and many other issues is participating in an exercise with Challenge Cards.

Challenge Cards: Considering Which Issues Resonate With You

Challenge Cards are available in many high school and post-secondary school career counsellor offices. Participating in the Challenge Cards exercise provides you with a fun way to evaluate which issues are important to you and see possible career options that match. There are a lot of issues and challenges to be tackled in the world. According to JP Michel, founder of Spark-Path who created the Challenge Cards, asking yourself which challenges you want to solve is a great way to help you focus on the impact you wish to make in the world. This can then lead you to the educational paths that will get you there.[23]

The idea of looking at challenges that you wish to solve is an interesting way to arrive at careers that might be of interest. Many guidance counsellors and career advisors use the Challenge Cards created by SparkPath. Each of the colourful cards includes a different challenge to solve on the front side. The recommended way to use the cards is to sort through them, taking some time to review each card and then place them into one of three piles: Very Interested, Interested, and Not Interested.

Once you have sorted the cards into piles, you choose three cards from your "Very Interested" pile. When you read the back of the cards, you will find a list of potential careers where people are currently working and applying their talents to solve these challenges. Challenge Cards are a great place to start your career exploration. Share with your family and friends the careers you have identified and ask them if they know anyone working on those challenges. Perhaps they could help you to set up an Informational Interview to find out more.

Here is a sample challenge card and the associated careers. Find out more at www.mysparkpath.com or ask your school guidance counsellor if they have the deck or access to the digital platform.

PROTECT
BIODIVERSITY AND
LANDSCAPE

Front of Challenge Card for "Protect Biodiversity and Landscape".

Protect Biodiversity and Landscape

Humans have the capability to conserve planet Earth's precious resources. Unfortunately, many of our systems, choices and habits hurt our environment in a number of ways. For example, through pollution, deforestation and overfishing, we have caused harm to ecosystems and animals.

Careers

- Water Quality Technicians
- Natural Scientists
- Wildlife Biologist
- Zoologist
- Paleontologist

- Climatologist
- Ecologist
- Geographer
- Meteorologists
- Oceanographer
- Conservation Biologist

Environmental efforts need to be more proactive in their protection work, rather than crisis-oriented. There are opportunities to research the best approaches for conserving the planet, for taking care of animals, for the development of nature reserves, for educating the public and for explaining the positive economic impact of effective environmental work.

mysparkpath.com

SPARKPATH

Back of Challenge Card for "Protect Biodiversity and Landscape".

Source: JP Michel, founder of SparkPath, received October 15th 2020, https://mysparkpath.com/

Get Excited About What You Want to Tackle!

Are you beginning to have an idea of what world challenges you wish to help solve? Is there something that is so important to you that you would love to work on solving it? Maybe you want to be involved in promoting the use of clean energy. Perhaps it is teaching children English in a developing country. Or perhaps you want to connect with lonely seniors, right where you live, locally.

You might need to take some time to reflect. I have some questions you can ask yourself that will help you uncover what issues are important to you. A variety of companies and non-profit organizations are already working on solving issues that you might find important. For instance, Patagonia is a company that supports environmental sustainability and is very active in protecting the earth.[24]

Step 8: Dreaming Big! What to Change in the World?

1. Considering the challenges that we are facing in the world today, list the ones you would like to address the most. Refer to the United Nations Sustainable Development Goals (SDGs) to generate ideas.

_____

_____

_____

_____

_____

_____

2. Are there certain people that are living in certain places that are facing issues that concern you? Consider describing the group of people you would like to help using demographics such as age, gender, ethnicity, or socio-economic status.

_____

_____

_____

3. What themes do you see in the world issues that you are drawn to solving? Conduct some online research to identify the organizations or companies that are currently working on addressing these issues and list them here:

_____

_____

_____

Great! You have identified some issues that are important to you and have found out which organizations are addressing these. You don't have to solve these issues alone, and perhaps there's already a team to which you can bring your passions, skills, and values.

Finding the Organizations That Tackle What You Value

We've already touched on social enterprises, but you can also consider where you would fit in working at companies, non-profits, or certified B Corporations. Through online research you can identify the organizations that are working on addressing the issues that matter to you. And it's not only social enterprises and non-profits, there is an increased awareness by executives at many companies to focus on defining their company mission; why they are in business and what is their impact on the world.

Leaders are becoming very clear on their company's values, or as author Simon Sinek would call it, their "why".[25] An organization's "why" inspires both their employees and their customers.

When you research companies, you will find that they are getting better at articulating their "why" and it may match with your "why". By understanding what is important to you, you can use this information as part of your career search, eliminating organizations that do not share your values. For instance, if environmental protection is an important value to you, conduct research to identify which firms include environmental sustainability as a key practice.

Companies like Nada Grocery or The Soap Dispensary are local grassroots companies that focus on improved sustainability in their own neighbourhood. Or perhaps you may wish to know more about companies that are making an impact globally such as Patagonia, Reformation, or Everlane.

When you visit the companies' websites, you can find out about their commitment to minimizing the impact on the environment. You'll see that these organizations share details about their manufacturing processes and how they source ingredients. They share that they invest in biodegradable packaging and focus on distributing their products while minimizing impact on the environment. All of these companies have roles that require different skills. Working at a company in a role that requires your skills and that aligns with your values will increase your job satisfaction. You'll begin to overlap circles in your *ikigai* diagram!

Non-profits are tackling issues

Non-profit organizations are often the first to come to mind when talking about who is solving key challenges. This is another workplace that you could bring what you are good at to address the issues that are important to you.

In fact, the non-profit sector is one of British Columbia's largest employers. There are 29,000 non-profit organizations, employing 66,000 full-time employees and 48,000 part-time employees.[26]

I would like to tell the story of Prerna, a young woman who saw an opportunity to bring together her skills and her values to work with a charity.

Prerna's Success Story:
Choosing Love

When you ask Prerna which social issues concern her, she says she is drawn to solving the refugee crisis. One day, she stumbled upon an organization with a unique solution to help refugees that she really admires, called Choose Love.

Choose Love has pop-up shops that sell products like kids' coats, winter boots, and sleeping bags. You choose to buy what you wish and then you "leave with nothing as each purchase you make is sent to someone who truly needs it."[27]

The organization has a very engaging website and social media. Prerna realized that this company employs graphic designers and content writers. And that is what Prerna is good at and loves to do! Working at this organization could be an opportunity for Prerna to do what she loves—with an organization that is providing what the world desperately needs.

Salary Myth-Busting

It is a common concern that the non-profit sector does not pay that well. However, let's review some research. Charity Village, a leading career destination and knowledge hub for the non-profit and charitable sectors, recently published the *2021 Canadian Non-profit Sector Salary and Benefits Report,* with results from 892 participating non-profit organizations. Charity Village found that in Canada, the average annual base compensation was $43,317 for support staff and $100,615 for senior executives. As with all career research it is important to conduct research for your geographic region, size of organization and job title to determine whether a career at a non-profit would meet your financial requirements.[28]

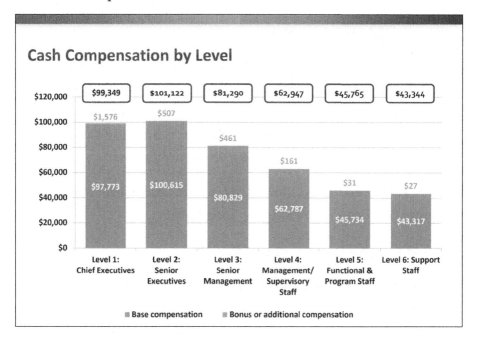

Source: Charity Village, "Introducing the 2021 Canadian Nonprofit Sector Salary and Benefits Report," 9, accessed May 18, 2021
https://charityvillage.com/introducing-the-2021-canadian-nonprofit-sector-salary-benefits-report/.

Consider Working at a Certified B Corporation

Certified

Corporation

Another type of organization designed around purpose and solving world challenges is the Certified B Corporation. These types of companies are required to participate in a certification process conducted by the non-profit B Lab. The certification is based on the company's performance on the B Impact Assessment. Certified B Corporations balance profit and purpose and meet the highest standards of social and environmental performance, transparency and legal accountability. These companies are part of a new movement seeing business as a force for good.[29] There are over 3,500 Certified B Corporations in over 70 countries. You can search for these companies at: www.bcorporation.net/directory.[30]

The World Needs YOU!

The world needs your talents and abilities. Remember, you have a lot to offer the world! We all have a role to play, similar to playing a specific part in an orchestra or a key position on a sports team. Your unique set of interests, talents, values, and the energy you bring are very much needed to make a difference.

A career that makes use of your skills and aligns with your values is also good for you in the long term.

Good for the World, Good For You

Happyologist, Gary Reker, a psychologist that lives in Canada, has published numerous books and articles on meaning and purpose in life. His research consistently shows that "finding meaning and purpose in life leads to happiness, not the other way around."[31]

You Are on a Mission!

Knowing yourself is just one piece of the puzzle. Contributing these skills and talents to meet what the world needs could lead you to that meaningful career or a "calling orientation".

You are just beginning your exploration. And remember, this is an ongoing process and you can pivot and alter your direction as you gather more information. For now, let's capture the information you have discovered about yourself so far and write it into a Personal Mission Statement.

Writing Your Personal Mission Statement

Your Personal Mission Statement is based on what you have already discovered about yourself throughout this book. It pulls together the positive changes you want to see more of in the world, your strengths, and your values all in one place. I developed my Personal Mission Statement by answering a few key questions.

What would you like to see more of in the world?
More young people living meaningful lives

What two strengths do you bring to solving this?
Positivity and Communication

What two values do you wish to see more of in the world?
Optimism and Fairness

Stephanie's Personal Mission Statement

I want to see
<u>more young people living meaningful lives</u>,

I will do this using my
<u>positivity and communication</u>

strengths so I can see more
<u>optimism and fairness</u> in the world.

Step 9: Develop Your Personal Mission Statement

What would you like to see more of in the world?

_____

What two strengths do you bring to solving this?

_____

What two values do you wish to see more of in the world?

_____

Fill in the blanks with your answers to complete your own Personal Mission Statement.

My Personal Mission Statement

I want to see

_____,

I will do this using my

_____and

_____

strengths so I can see more

_____and

_____

in the world.

Summary

In this chapter, "What the World Needs", the exercises you completed were aimed at identifying the world issues that you feel are important to address. You might have connected to one of the United Nations Sustainable Development Goals. Or if your school has the Challenge Cards, you might have identified a key issue to solve. Or you may have identified another concern to take on.

In any case, the world needs you. You are unique with your own dreams, set of values, and your own personal mission. Take time to add this newly-discovered information to your *ikigai* diagram—circle three, "What the World Needs" at the back of this book.

We all have a role to play in making this world a better place. There are so many issues and challenges to take on and some will resonate with you more than others. Applying your talents and skills to working on the issues that are important to you will give your life meaning and provide a purpose or direction to your life. You may need to take some time to reflect and uncover where you wish to apply your energy. And once you have a sense of your "why", this will provide you with sustained motivation and drive.

In the next chapter, we'll cover the fourth circle in the *ikigai* model, "What You Can be Paid For". How do you find those meaningful careers that would allow you to do what you love, do what you are good at, and address what the world needs—all while allowing you financial independence?

To uncover the careers that you can be paid for, I will share how to find information on workplace trends and salaries. This information, combined with what you have discovered about yourself, will allow you to develop a targeted list of careers to explore that you will be excited to pursue.

Checklist

☐ Dream Big! Outline the challenges you wish to address in the world

☐ Write your Personal Mission Statement

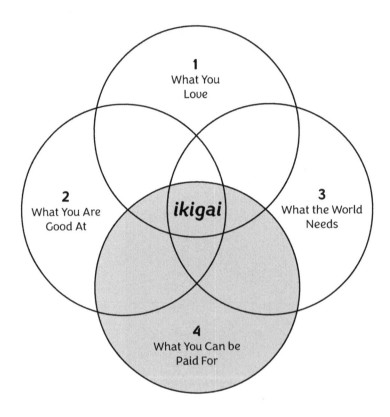

CHAPTER 4

What You Can be Paid For

In the last few chapters, you were asked to identify what you love, what you are good at, and what the world needs. This provided you with some of the details to fill out circles one, two, and three of your *ikigai* diagram. Remember that your *ikigai* diagram is your guide. It includes information about you and is a touchstone that you can refer to when evaluating which careers are a fit.

The last key to a meaningful career is a role that includes paying you so you can be financially independent. To find such roles, you need to know which careers and skills will be in demand and the associated training that is required. This will ensure you are in a good position when you graduate.

In this chapter, you will answer questions to aid in filling out circle four "What You Can be Paid For" on your *ikigai* diagram. The aim is to identify careers that will allow you to do what you love, use your talents (do what you are good at), and aim your talents at addressing what the world needs, all while ensuring financial independence. The intersection of all four circles will inform your meaningful career journey.

To begin, let's look into the future to see what careers are forecasted to be in demand and what training is required so that you will be well-positioned. No matter which career you plan to pursue, most will require some additional training. You might be required to obtain new knowledge and training over the next few years. This requires that you research the career trends and the skills that will be in demand in the future, *before* you begin your training so that the investment of your time and money prepares you for success. The good news is that there are organizations that research future trends in the labour market that you can easily tap into.

Labour Market Information

There are many sources of labour market information outlining the careers and skills that will be in demand. In British Columbia (BC), this information is found at the government website www.workbc.ca where you can find the Work BC Labour Market Outlook: 2019 Edition.[32] This report has statistics on which careers are predicted to be in demand and which careers are forecasted to experience a slowing down of demand.

So, which type of jobs will be in demand? The Work BC Labour Market Outlook: 2019 Edition report forecasts the number of job openings by major occupational groups and details salary information for them. For BC, the top occupational groups, ranked highest for job openings are: Sales and Service; Business, Finance and Administration; Management; and Trades, Transport and Equipment Operators and Related. Some of the growth is being driven by openings and some of it by retirements of current workers.[33] These might be career categories that are of interest to you.

Job Openings of Major Industry Group BC, 2019-2029

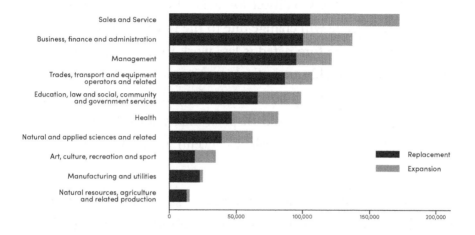

Source: *Province of British Columbia, British Columbia Labour Market Outlook: 2019 Edition Report, accessed June 10th, 2020, 19, https://www.workbc.ca/Labour-Market-Industry/Labour-Market-Outlook.aspx.*

The Future of Work: Technology Leads the Fourth Industrial Revolution

The workplace is changing so quickly! The fourth industrial revolution includes the expanded use of robots, process automation, machine learning, and artificial intelligence. These technologies will have an effect on business processes and researchers are looking to see what the future impacts will be on human capital. What we do know is that the coming fourth industrial revolution will disrupt some industries. While it is a new chapter in human development, enabled by extraordinary technology advances, it is comparable to the first, second, and third industrial revolutions. How? It is a merging of the physical, digital, and biological worlds in ways that create both huge promise and potential peril.[34] As you embark on your career, it is important to consider how current jobs will be affected and what future jobs will look like. What will the future of work look like?

The Impact of Technology on Jobs

Deloitte and the Coalition for Education have studied how the work landscape will change due to the fourth industrial revolution. One change forecasted is less work for people, which will move us more quickly to a gig-based economy, meaning more people will be working on contracts. According to the study, emerging technologies could displace many jobs, however it is forecasted that most job loss will be concentrated in the low-middle skill jobs.[35]

However, "despite projected heavy job displacement, the Canadian economy is expected to add 2.4 million jobs over four years, all requiring a new mix of skills."[36]

Skills that will be In Demand

So, what skills are forecasted to be in demand? Royal Bank of Canada (RBC) conducted a study, listening to over 5,000 Canadians on how Canada can prepare for a disruption, and generated a report bringing together the perspectives of educators, employers, and youth on the impacts of the skills revolution.

Forecasted in the RBC, *Bridging the Gap* report, "virtually all job openings will place significant importance on judgment and decision making and more than two thirds will value an ability to manage people and resources."[37] Are these skills you already have or can develop?

According to the "Projected Skills Demand for All Occupations" included in the RBC Humans Wanted report, "the strongest demand is for the foundational skills that separate good from great in every walk of life, and especially in Canada's increasingly services-oriented economy. **Communication, emotional intelligence, critical thinking, analysis:** young Canadians will need these skills in an age of rapid change. They will need to work well with an increasingly diverse range of other people—business partners from around the world, plus co-workers of all ages, genders, languages and cultures—and to complement technology, which will become ever more pervasive."[38]

While you are preparing for your career, keep in mind the skills required in the future so you will be positioned, using a Canadian reference, where "the hockey puck is going".

Develop your Career Exploration Plan

I would like you to create a list of careers to explore. You may already have some job titles in mind from reviewing the United Nations Sustainable Development Goals or if you participated in the Challenge Cards exercise. If you are still looking, I have included some careers to review listed in two tables: the O*NET Occupational Interest Table and the Skilled Trades Table.[39] First, let's review some occupation categories.

Which Categories Sound Like You?

Step 10: Occupation Categories for Consideration

In the O*NET Occupational Interest Table on the next page, review and then select the occupation categories that sound like you.

O*NET Occupational Interest Table[40]

Occupation Categories	Interested?
Hands-on: Realistic occupations frequently involve work activities that include practical, hands-on problems and solutions. They often deal with plants, animals, and real-world materials like wood, tools, and machinery. Many of the occupations require working outside and do not involve a lot of paperwork or working closely with others.	
Social: Social occupations usually involve working with, communicating with, and teaching people. These occupations often involve helping or providing service to others.	
Investigative: Investigative occupations typically include working with ideas and require an extensive amount of thinking. These occupations can involve searching for facts and figuring out problems mentally.	
Enterprising: Enterprising occupations are often comprised of starting up and carrying out projects. These occupations can involve leading people and making many decisions. Sometimes they require risk-taking and they often deal with business.	

Artistic: Artistic occupations often require working with forms, designs, and patterns. They typically require self-expression and the work can be done without following a clear set of rules.	
Routinized: Routinized occupations frequently require following set procedures and routines. These occupations can include working with data and details more than with ideas. Usually there is a clear line of authority to follow.	

Source: This page includes information from the https://www.onetcenter.org/tools.html O*NET Career Exploration Tools by the U.S. Department of Labor, Employment and Training Administration (USDOL/ETA). Used under the https://creativecommons.org/licenses/by-nd/4.0/ CC BY-ND 4.0 license. O*NET® is a trademark of USDOL/ETA.

Step 11: Circle the Careers of Interest from the O*Net Occupational Interest Table

Next, in the O*Net Occupational Interest Table on the next page, circle the careers that you would like to investigate further from the occupational categories that sound like you. You can add these careers to your Career Exploration Plan coming up next in this chapter.

O*Net Occupational Interest Table [40]

HANDS-ON "Practical, hands-on"	• Electrical and Electronics Engineers • Aerospace Engineers • Cooks • Carpenters • Automotive Service Technician • Electricians • Electronic Service Technicians • Welders • Painters • Drivers • Heavy Duty Equipment Mechanics • Material Handlers • Heavy Equipment Operators • General Farm Workers
SOCIAL "Working with and helping people"	• Teachers • Social Workers • Family, Marriage and other related Counselors • Professional Occupations in Religion • Post-Secondary Teaching and Research Assistants • Physiotherapists • Educational Counselors • Occupational Therapist • Early Childhood Educators and Assistants • Licensed Practical Nurses • Massage Therapists • Paramedical Occupations • Practitioners of Natural Healing • Nurse Aides, Orderlies and Patients Service Associates • Food and Beverage Servers
ARTISTIC "Design and self-expression"	• Teachers • Producers, Directors, Choreographers and Related Occupations • Web Designers and Developers • Musicians and Singers • Authors and Writers • Painters, Sculptures, and other Visual Artists • Architects • Editors • Actors and Comedians • Journalists • Urban and Land-Use Planners • Early Childhood Educators • Graphic Designers and Illustrators • Drafting Technologists • Interior Designers and Interior Decorators

INVESTIGATIVE "Thinking and working with ideas"	• Computer Programmers and Interactive Media Developers • Software Engineers and Designers • Civil Engineers • General Practitioners and Family Physicians • Electrical and Electronics Engineers • Specialist Physicians • Mechanical Engineers • Pharmacists • Biologists and related Scientists • Dentists • Psychologists • Geoscientists and Oceanographers • Dietitians and Nutritionists • Urban and Land Use Planners • Industrial and Manufacturing Engineers
ENTERPRISING "Business and risk-taking"	• Retail and Wholesale Trade Managers • Restaurant and Food Service Managers • Construction Managers • Corporate Sales Managers • Manufacturing Managers • Real Estate Agents and Salespersons • Chefs • Retail Sales Supervisors • Insurance Agents and Brokers • Retail and Wholesale Buyers • Conference and Event Planners • Retail Salespersons • Sales and Representatives- Wholesale Trade (Non-Technical) • Tour and Travel Guides • Outdoor Sport and Recreational Guides
ROUTINIZED "Established rules and procedures"	• Financial Auditors and Accountants • Database Analysts and Data Administrators • Librarians • Administrative Officers and Assistants • Accounting Technicians and Bookkeepers • Executive Assistant • Office Support Workers • Receptionists • Accounting and Related Clerks • Storekeepers and Parts Persons • Data Entry Clerks • Casino Occupations • Survey Interviewers and Statistical Clerks • Cashiers • Store Shelf Stockers, Clerks and Order Fillers

Meaningful Careers in the Skilled Trades

When thinking about meaningful careers, the skilled trades are a great option to consider. There are over 95 trades to choose from according to the Canadian Industry Training Authority (ITA). Skilled Trades offer opportunities to fully fulfill your *ikigai*: doing something you love, doing something you are good at, meeting the needs of your community, and being well-paid.

Certified tradespeople are in high demand around the world.[41] There are a few categories listed on www.youth.itabc.ca that might help you discover a trade that appeals to you. The categories are: Outdoorists, Operators, Artisans, Analyzers, Builders, and Fixers.

Outdoorists

Outdoorists are in their element when in the outdoors. Are you adventurous, curious, nimble? Some trades to consider include arborist technician or landscape horticulturalist. An arborist technician takes care of trees and the surrounding environment and often work for parks departments, the city, contractors, or are possibly self-employed.[42] A landscape horticulturist means you spend time outside, perhaps working at one place, or you might work for an employer and work at many sites developing and maintaining green spaces.[43]

Operators

Operators are calm, coordinated, and decisive. A crane operator means working for construction, industrial, mining, and railway companies. According to itabc.ca you can earn an annual salary of $65,000 CAD.[44] Heavy equipment operators are also included under the category of Operators and they operate bulldozers, backhoes, loaders. Heavy equipment operators might work for construction companies, public works departments, logging, and cargo handling companies, with an annual salary of $66,000 - $95,000 CAD according to itabc.ca.[45]

Artisans

The Artisan category includes careers such as baker, cook, dairy production technician, funeral director, hairstylist, meat-cutter, and painter and decorator. "Artisans are attentive, creative, expressive, inventive and precise".[46] Demand for cooks is one of the highest according to the BC Labour Market Outlook 2019 study with 12,200 job openings projected between 2019-2029.[47]

Analyzers

The Analyzer category includes the following trades: instrumentation and control technician, marine service technician, plumber, refrigeration and A/C mechanic, sprinkler system installer, steamfitter/pipefitter. People in these roles are agile, independent, inquisitive, logical, and persistent.[48]

Builders

The Builder category includes many trades that might be of interest to you and include the following: cabinetmaker, carpenter, domestic/commercial gasfitter, construction electrician, glazier, ironworker, machinist, metal fabricator (fitter), residential steep roofer, sheet metal worker and welder.[49] A career as a Builder might appeal to you if you can see the big picture and love the details. You would be well suited if you are athletic, collaborative, mathematical, precise, and tactile.[50]

Fixers

And last, the Fixer category of trade careers includes the following trades roles: aircraft maintenance technician, automotive service technician, heavy duty equipment technician, industrial electrician, industrial mechanic (millwright), motor vehicle body repairer, motorcycle mechanic, and truck and transport mechanic.[51] "Fixers tend to be analytical, dexterous, mechanical, resourceful, and systematic."[52]

What Does Education Look Like For Skilled Trades?

Additional training is required for success in these careers and sometimes training can begin in high school. A trade apprenticeship allows you to learn the trade through a combination of classroom training and work-based training.

Often, the classroom education consists of about 6-8 weeks per year and the rest of the year is spent training on the job while getting paid. It usually takes about four years to complete an apprenticeship.

Obtaining your trade ticket or certificate of qualification allows you to work anywhere in BC and possibly in other provinces, depending on the trade. There are 50 Red Seal trades and obtaining the Red Seal credential will facilitate you working in most provinces in Canada.[53]

Step 12: Circle the Careers of Interest from the Skilled Trades Table

Review the Skilled Trades Table and circle any careers that you would like to investigate further. Add them to your Career Exploration Plan.

Skilled Trades Table

OUTDOORIST "Adventurous, curious, nimble, outdoorsy and visual"	• Arborist Technician	• Landscape Horticulturist
OPERATOR "Calm, careful, confident, coordinated, and decisive"	• Heavy Equipment Operator	• Crane Operator
ARTISAN "Attentive, creative, expressive, and inventive"	• Baker • Cook • Dairy Production Technician	• Funeral Director • Hairstylist • Meatcutter • Painter and Decorator
ANALYZER "Agile, independent, inquisitive, logical, and persistent"	• Instrumentation and Control Technician • Marine Service Technician • Plumber	• Refrigeration and A/C Mechanic • Sprinkler System Installer • Steamfitter/Pipefitter
BUILDER "Athletic, collaborative, mathematical, precise and tactile"	• Cabinetmaker • Carpenter • Domestic/Commercial Gasfitter • Construction Electrician • Glazier • Ironworker	• Machinist • Metal Fabricator (Fitter) • Residential Steep Roofer • Sheet Metal Worker • Welder
FIXER "Analytical, dexterous, mechanical, resourceful, and systematic"	• Aircraft Maintenance Technician • Automotive Service Technician • Heavy Duty Equipment Technician	• Industrial Electrician • Industrial Mechanic (Millwright) • Motor Vehicle Body Repair • Motorcycle Mechanic • Truck and Transport Mechanic

Source: "Find Your Trade: What Are You Made Of?", ITA Youth, accessed January 31, 2021, https://youth. itabc.ca/trade-finder/

Here is an opportunity for you to list the careers that you are interested in exploring futher.

Step 13: Develop Your Career Exploration Plan

List of Careers to Explore

Now that you have your list of potential careers to explore, add these careers to circle four of your *ikigai* diagram at the back of this book. Remember, your *ikigai* diagram is fluid and changeable. You may add or remove careers to your diagram as you find out more information about what these careers are really like.

Now What? Next Steps in Researching Your Careers

The next step is conducting research to determine whether the careers on your list are good-paying careers, whether or not these careers will be in demand when you graduate, and which careers are a fit for you.

I have three research strategy tips for finding out more information about your list of careers:

Three Research Strategy Tips

1: Conduct online research. There are many online resources that provide information on which careers will be in demand, including salary information and educational requirements. Some of these sites are government websites. In British Columbia, the government website www.workbc.ca provides this information. Google and LinkedIn can also be great online sources.

2: Conduct Informational Interviews. Consider speaking to someone that is currently in the role to arrange an Informational Interview with them.

3: Connect to an Industry Association. Search for the industry association in the field you are interested in to find out more about that career. You can join as a student and subscribe to the association newsletter.

Let's go into more detail for these approaches.

1. Conduct Online Research

Government Websites

A great online resource to find out about different careers is found at the government of British Columbia website: www.workbc.ca.[54] There are 500 career profiles available to search. You can search by job title, keywords or NOC (National Occupational Classification). Let's reflect on this through Kyle's experience.

Kyle's Success Story:
Finding a Career in the Woods

Kyle is a Grade 12 student interested in becoming a conservation officer. In working on his *ikigai* diagram, he has realized that he loves to be outdoors in nature and values protecting the environment. He feels the world needs to protect the environment for future generations. The role of conservation officer seems to fit with the information on his *ikigai* diagram so far.

Kyle would like to find out more about this career, what it pays, and whether it is in demand so he visited the website: www.workbc.ca. Kyle searched for the job title that matches with "conservation officer" and found the job title of "Conservation and Fishery Officers" where he found graphs stating the annual provincial median salary, the provincial hourly rate and the labour market outlook.

Earnings

Annual provincial median salary

$72,996

Source: 2020 Job Bank Wage Data

Note: Estimated median employment income based on 2020 Job Bank median hourly wage rate (median annual salary = hourly wage rate x 40 (hours per week) x 52.14 (weeks per year)).

Provincial hourly rate

High	$40.00/hr
Median	$35.00/hr
Low	$21.63/hr

Source: 2020 Job Bank Wage Report

BC Labour Market

Provincial Outlook

Forecasted average employment growth rate

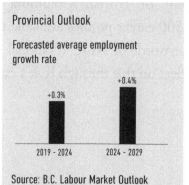

+0.3%   2019 - 2024
+0.4%   2024 - 2029

Source: B.C. Labour Market Outlook

Source: Work BC, "Conservation and Fishery Officers (NOC 2224)," Province of British Columbia, accessed February 19, 2020, https://www.workbc.ca/Jobs-Careers/Explore-Careers/Browse-Career-Profile/2224.

The occupational skills required for the conservation officer role are speaking and active listening. Kyle acknowledges that he has developed these communications skills while participating in his school improvisational theatre program and as a delegate in the Model United Nations events. It looks like this is a career that Kyle will pursue further.

For more information on a day in the life of a variety of career roles, seek out the over 140 WorkBC Career Trek videos found at www.careertrekbc.ca. The video on the conservation and fishery officers was very informative for Kyle!

More Online Research Sources

Google

Google is a great resource and can lead to a lot of information on careers. For instance, you can google the United Nations SDG you are interested in solving. If you selected Goal #2 which is "Zero Hunger", you can conduct a google search of "Zero Hunger Organizations" and you will find a list of organizations that are working on solving this issue. From there, select a company and explore their website to find out more about their mission and who works there. Find out about individuals that work at these companies and their career paths through LinkedIn.

LinkedIn

If you have a LinkedIn account (to be discussed later in this book) you can search for a profile of an individual that you have found at a company of interest and review the employee's career journey. You will also be able to see the type of education that they have completed. You can use LinkedIn to search for organizations that are solving the challenges you are interested in, too.

For example, type "Zero Hunger Organizations" in the search tool and see which people and organizations come up.

2. Conduct Informational Interviews

Another way to find out information about the careers listed on your Career Exploration Plan is speaking to someone already working in that career. You can arrange a virtual meeting or meet in person to find out more details on the career. This is called an Informational Interview.

How do you find those working in the careers you are interested in? Well, we talked about finding profiles on LinkedIn. You can message them asking for an Informational Interview. Another avenue is determining if you already know a family member working in one of the occupations on your list. Or ask your friends if they know of anyone. If they do know someone, ask them to introduce you via email or even by text. Follow up and arrange a 20-minute meeting to chat with them about their career. During the chat, you can ask them how they got into their role and what they like or dislike about their job. You can also find out the education, knowledge, and skills required to be successful in that career.

If you can, ask them if they would recommend someone else you could speak with. This way you are getting to connect with one more person and when you meet with that new person ask the same thing. I like to call it the hop-hop approach!

Informational Interviews are quite a common practice in Canada. Most people are very open and willing to take the time to meet with you and share their experience.

For this exercise, list who you know that is working in the careers that you are interested in. Add their name to your Informational Interview Contact Plan.

Step 14: Informational Interview Contact Plan

List the careers you are interested in and the names of people you know that are working in these careers. Find out their contact information and add this to the chart.

Career	Name	Contact Info

Set a goal to contact two or three people for a call or virtual meeting to find out more about these careers. Some sample questions to ask might include:

- How did you become interested in this career?

- What do you most enjoy about your work?

- What do you least enjoy about your work?

- What advice would you give to someone interested in pursuing this as a career?

- Are there any industry associations that you would recommend I join?

- What are the typical educational requirements for someone entering into this career?

- Would you choose this career again if you knew what you know now?

When you are at an Informational Interview, you are asking questions about getting into a career. Understand that these interviews don't automatically lead to a job, but sometimes you can get lucky! This happened to a student of mine, Cat.

Cat's Success Story:
She Shoots, She Scores

Cat was a student in a business management program and dreamed of working in sports marketing with a team like the Canucks. Cat had shared that desire with me. When an industry event came up that featured executives speaking from the Canucks, I suggested to Cat that she attend, and, if possible, after the event introduce herself to the speaker and thank them for speaking.

It turned out that Cat did just that and was able to follow up with the speaker to arrange an Informational Interview. This led to some key introductions at the head office that eventually led to Cat being hired into the organization.

You might learn from your Informational Interviews that additional education is required for the career you are interested in. Keep track of this and we will explore how to find the right program and school in the next chapter.

3. Connect to Industry Associations

There are associations for every industry profession you can think of. There are international, national, provincial and city-wide associations. In business, there are boards of trade, chambers of commerce, accounting associations, marketing associations, public relations societies, and associations for the supply and logistics industry.

So how do you find an association in the industry you are interested in? You can search on Google and LinkedIn, or you can find a fairly comprehensive list of Canadian Industry Associations at www.cpmdq.com/htm/org.canada2.htm.

Once you find an association of interest, visit their website and have a look at the event listings and activities. Consider joining as a student member or volunteering on a committee. If available, sign up for the e-newsletter and you will receive details on events, activities, and sometimes job postings, right into your inbox.

For the next activity, please conduct some online research to identify the associations for the careers you are interested in. List the associations in the table in Step 15 on the next page. Set some goals to either attend an event, join as a student member, volunteer, or sign up for the association's newsletter.

Step 15: Prepare Your List of Associations

Name of Association	Attend an Event	Join as a member	Volunteer	Sign up for a newsletter

Summary

In chapter four, called "What You Can be Paid For", the goal was to identify careers for further exploration and research. When you determine ahead of time the careers that will be in demand, you have information that will allow you to position yourself well upon graduation. Researching the salary ranges of the careers of interest allows you to evaluate how well the careers pay.

Your Career Exploration Plan might include career ideas that came to you by reviewing the UN Sustainable Development Goals or by participating in a Challenge Cards exercise. Or perhaps you added some careers to your list selected from either the O*Net Occupational Interest Table or the Skilled Trades Table.

Your research findings in this chapter provide you with the information to determine what you can get paid for and if a career is a good fit. Be sure to add your list of careers from your Career Exploration Plan to circle four of your *ikigai* diagram at the back of this book.

In this chapter, you were also introduced to three strategic research approaches to find out about the careers on your list. The goal is to determine if the careers on your list are a fit, will be in demand in the future, and their forecasted salaries.

Tip #1 outlined how to conduct online research through accessing government websites and using Google and LinkedIn to find salary information and skills in demand.

Tip #2 suggested you meet with someone that is already working in the role you are interested in and speak with them directly by conducting an Informational Interview.

Tip #3 suggested you connect with industry associations to find out how to attend an event, become a student member, volunteer, and/or sign up for the e-newsletter.

Lastly, it is most likely that any career of interest will require additional training. The next step is to find out how to identify the educational programs and the institutions that offer this training. There are several ways to find this out and that will be covered in the next chapter.

Checklist

☐ Review: The O*NET Occupational Interest Table

☐ Review: The Skilled Trades Table

☐ Develop your Career Exploration Plan outlining a list of careers

☐ Conduct research on careers of interest

1: Conduct Online Research

☐ Visit websites like workbc.ca to assess demand, salary information, and the credentials required

☐ Use Google and LinkedIn to research companies and individuals

2: Conduct Informational Interviews

☐ Develop your Informational Interview Contact Plan

3: Connect to Industry Associations

☐ Attend an event

☐ Join as a student member

☐ Volunteer

☐ Subscribe to the association's e-newsletter

CHAPTER 5

What Education Do You Need?

In the previous chapter, "What Can You be Paid For", the focus was on conducting research about the careers listed on your Career Exploration Plan. You were introduced to three strategic research tips and the goals of your research were to determine: which careers could be a fit; the forecasted demand for each career, and predicted, potential salaries.

After doing these exercises, you added the careers you were interested into circle four of your *ikigai* diagram. But while you were conducting your research, did you find out that you will need to gain additional education or training?

Most jobs do require some form of additional training after high school. It is forecasted that there will be 861,000 job openings in BC between 2019 and 2029 as reported in the British Columbia Labour Market Outline Study, 2019.[55] Of those future jobs, 36% of these will require either a bachelor's, graduate or professional degree. And, another 41% of the job openings are expected to require either a diploma, certificate, or apprenticeship training.

Job Openings by Education BC 2019-2029

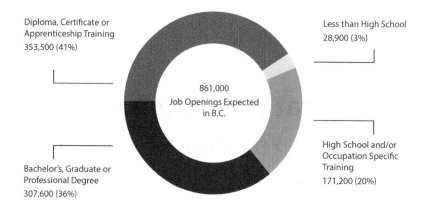

Diploma, Certificate or Apprenticeship Training
353,500 (41%)

Less than High School
28,900 (3%)

861,000
Job Openings Expected
in B.C.

Bachelor's, Graduate or Professional Degree
307,600 (36%)

High School and/or Occupation Specific Training
171,200 (20%)

Source: Province of British Columbia, British Columbia Labour Market Outlook: 2019 Edition Report, accessed June 10th, 2020, 12, https://www.workbc.ca/Labour-Market-Industry/Labour-Market-Outlook.aspx.

So it is anticipated that you will need to consider enrolling in additional post-secondary or apprenticeship training for the careers you might be interested in. We know that future earnings are tied to the demand for certain careers. Additional training and certification can also play a role in determining your future earnings.

More Training = Higher Earnings

A 2017 study by Statistics Canada highlighted that further training pays off in earnings. That training may be skilled trades certifications or post-secondary education. The report stated that "men with an apprenticeship certificate, had particularly high earnings in 2015. This reflected the strong demand in the labour market for these workers overall. The median earnings were $72,955, and these men earned 31% more than men with high school as their highest educational qualification, 7% more than men with a college diploma, but 11% less than men with a bachelor's degree."[56]

In addition, the report indicated that "the earnings of women with a bachelor's degree were 58% higher than the earnings of women with a high school diploma and 41% higher than the earnings of women with college education."[57]

The right type of education and training can have a positive effect on the salary you will earn, so you want to make a good choice—studying is an investment of both your time and your money.

If you are interested, you can review research on salaries by field of study. The 2016 Statistics Canada report called, *Earnings of Postsecondary Graduates by Detailed Field of Study*, includes Canadian salaries, broken down by gender and by education levels such as college, bachelor's degree, and master's degree. Completing different degrees provides different potential earnings advantages. For instance, the findings indicate that the highest paid bachelor's degree graduates are male graduates in management sciences and qualitative methods.[58]

According to an RBC article listing the top ten most valuable degrees in Canada, are:[59]

1. Business aka management sciences average salary $110,000-$115,000

2. Petroleum or chemical engineering average salary $104,000

3. Finance average salary $103,376

4. Pharmacology average salary $102,398

5. Geosciences average salary $100,006

6. Software engineering average salary $90,001

7. Business administration average salary $85,508

8. Specialized engineering average salary $85,009

9. Nursing average salary $84,510

10. Civil engineering average salary $80,080

Average salaries stated in 2017 dollars

If you found out during your career exploration research that you will need further education, then the next step is to identify the programs and the schools that offer the credentials you will require. You want to ensure you enroll in the program that will help you prepare for the career you wish to pursue.

Many students don't take the steps to determine the type of certificate, diploma, or degree they will require for certain careers. Or students enroll in a program that may not prepare them for a career.

In fact, a 2019 study of over 11,000 people across the world asked participants about their higher education experience and whether or not it prepared them for their career. Of the Canadians in the survey, 42% of the respondents stated that their higher education did not prepare them for their careers.[60] It is unclear whether people felt they were not prepared because, upon graduation, they chose to work in a field that they did not study for, or that their university program did not prepare them for their career.[61]

However, the fact that 42% of students surveyed felt that their education did not prepare them for their careers seems to mean that those students invested time and money in programs that did not lead them somewhere specific.

So why does this happen? It happens because students are often told that they will figure it out once they are in college or university. And sometimes they do. However, education takes time and money. I think students graduate unprepared for careers because students aren't encouraged to begin with an end in mind. I know this first-hand, because that is what I did.

It Happened to Me

If you recall, after my first year in university, I transferred into the psychology program from the science program and when I was in my 3rd year, was asked by a friend, "What are you going to do when you graduate?"

I was shocked by this question! I did not have an answer. I had no idea if the psychology degree I was pursuing would lead me to a job or not. I found out then and there, from my friend, that if I wanted a career working in the field of psychology, I would have to enroll in further study to obtain a master's degree or a PhD.

This was the first I had heard of this! I wanted to know, was this the only path for me? I did not have this option in mind. In fact, I didn't have any options in mind. When I switched to pursue a psychology degree, I definitely did not begin with an end in mind.

So, what would I have done differently? I would have started with some backward design.

Backward Design: Start With The End in Mind

Gina Shereda, in her article called *Backward Design Your Way to a Fulfilling Career*, states that if you can take the time to "think about your desired outcomes early in your career, you will save yourself time." She says she wishes that she had been more intentional while in graduate school, as she might have more quickly identified the fulfilling aspects of her work.[62]

And that is exactly the reason behind writing this book. The goal is to help you reflect and understand more about yourself and the job market, informing your decision on what education is required.

Your career interests are based on the amazing, thoughtful reflections you have done so far and entered into your personal *ikigai* diagram. You have discovered what you love, what you are good at, and what the world needs. Plus, through your online research, meeting with people in Informational Interviews and by connecting to industry associations, you now have a shortened list of careers to explore further that are a possible fit for you.

Through your research, you have discovered that to achieve success in any of the careers you have identified, you need to enroll in education that brings you the required knowledge and credentials. The next step is identifying the programs and the schools that offer them. You can do this through a few methods. Let me share them with you.

Finding the Programs and the Schools

Government Websites

A great online resource is the Career Explore website found at www.workbc.ca.[63] Here you can find out the post-secondary programs for the careers that you might be interested in.

Remember Kyle from Chapter 4? He was interested in pursuing a career as a conservation officer.

Kyle conducted online research and visited the helpful website www.educationplannerbc.ca to find the programs that prepare you for a career as a conservation officer. He found eleven post-secondary institutions offering programs to explore further. Some of these programs were offered at Vancouver Island University, British Columbia Institute of Technology, and the University of Victoria in British Columbia.

Kyle reviewed each school's program details and decided which programs to apply to. He reviewed the application requirements and submitted his application to the programs he was interested in. Requirements varied—some of the applications required that he provide character references, a personal profile, and a resume.

Because each program's requirements are different, be sure to read each school's website information carefully. When you begin with an end in mind you ensure that you will be spending your money and your time effectively. You will be working towards meeting the educational requirements for a career that you have researched and that you are interested in.

In addition to www.educationplannerbc.ca, you can use these other resources to locate programs and schools:

www.schoolfinder.com

This website is a go-to destination for Canadian students. Here, you can search for schools, programs, and careers. You can even create a free profile to get matched automatically with schools and programs.[64] And for international students that wish to study in Canada, the company supports the platform called StudyinCanada.com where students can create a free profile and be matched with programs, schools, and careers in Canada.[65]

Applying To Schools

When to Apply

You typically apply to schools in the fall, as early as October for some schools. You apply the year prior to the year you wish to attend. If accepted, you would begin your studies in September of the following year. Some schools may have several application intakes and start dates, so be sure to check websites carefully.

School Considerations

Living On/Off Campus or at Home

There are a lot of factors to consider when researching schools and programs. When considering different schools, would you prefer a "campus university"? A campus university has everything located on one site, including the teaching facilities, accommodation, food services, and workout amenities. A "city university" might suit you better if you are looking to connect to life outside of your institution or if you need to work part-time. Or if you wish to rent an apartment or share a flat off campus. Some universities can provide you with an international experience while you study in global cities such as London, England or Sydney, Australia.[66] Or perhaps you may wish to study at a local school and have the option to live at home while you study.

Extracurricular Activities

Consider what extracurricular activities you may wish to participate in. Determine if there are volunteer opportunities posted on the website. See if there are sports, clubs, and societies available that match your interests.

Review University Rankings

You might consider reviewing the rankings if that is of interest to you to see where your future school ranks in the world.

In Canada, we are very lucky to have several universities ranked in the top 100 in the world. According to the "Times Higher Education, World University Rankings for 2021", the University of Toronto places 18th, the University of British Columbia places 34th, McGill in Montreal is 40th on the list, McMaster University which is located in Hamilton is ranked 69th, and the University of Montreal ranks 73rd in the world.[67]

This website, www.timeshighereducation.com, also has a search function to help you find which schools offer programs of interest to you in other countries.

Finding Out More: Visit School Websites and Connect Via Social Media

Part of figuring out which programs to apply to includes determining which school you wish to attend. There is great value in visiting school websites to find out more about their programs, the admission requirements, and their due dates. You can also follow a school's social media accounts.

If you want to get a feel for a school's campus and facilities, many schools have virtual tour videos posted so you can see the campus before visiting in person. If you can, a physical visit to a school allows you to "imagine" yourself on campus, and helps orient you to the size and facilities available. During on-campus visits, you can meet with faculty, students, and even former students (alumni), to get additional insights into your program of interest and the job opportunities that follow.

You can visit campuses on your own without an appointment, or you can keep an eye out and schedule your visit during the on-campus open houses. Or, you could apply first, and then once you have applied to a school, you might be invited to attend on-campus events. Here is an example of an invitation from the University of Victoria.[68]

You're invited to join us for Explore UVic on Saturday, February 1, 2020, to see if UVic really is the perfect fit for your goals, values, and wildest dreams.

Explore UVic is a fun-filled day created especially for high school and transfer students who are hoping to learn more about the University of Victoria. A few of the highlights include:

- an information and faculty fair with representatives from academic programs, co-op, financial aid, residence services, food services, and more

- student experience panels with current UVic students

- an overview presentation of the admission process and your next steps (separate presentations for future applicants, grade 12 applicants, and transfer students)

- campus tours and faculty-based building tours of your future classrooms and labs

- exciting sample lectures from outstanding professors

- free on-campus parking

- free bus transportation from Swartz Bay and back if you're taking the ferry

For more information and to register, please visit the event page. Register Here!

From: Student Recruitment Officer, University of Victoria

Finding out More: Speak to Students Already Attending a School/Program of Interest

Wouldn't it be great if you could speak to a student in the program that you are considering while you were browsing a school's website from home?

There is a new platform that allows you to do just that. Diego Fanara is the founder of Unibuddy: "I started Unibuddy because I couldn't decide which university to go to based on websites and brochures alone. Making a decision without access to first-hand information is really difficult. The questions I really wanted to answer were: *What's it really like to study there? Will I meet people like me?* The sort of things only a current student could answer. And so, knowing that hearing from our peers is key to decision making, Unibuddy was born!"[69]

Unibuddy connects prospective students to current university students and staff, providing them with the information needed to decide where to go to university and what to study.[70]

University of Guelph is a Canadian school that uses the Unibuddy platform, allowing both potential domestic and international students to chat with student ambassadors and staff.[71]

To find schools that are using the Unibuddy platform go to: www.unibuddy.com/for-students.

Program Considerations

There are several major factors to consider about the program you are applying to such as: identifying the admission requirements, and details like program length, whether it prepares you for a future career, and whether the program offers cooperative education options. This last offering would provide opportunities for you to gain paid work experience during one or more school semesters.[72] It might be important to you to identify if the program you are interested in offers international exchange opportunities as well.

All of these factors will play into your decision making. Another major consideration is the overall cost of your education.

Financial Considerations

Paying for your Education

There are many costs to pay when you become a post-secondary student and you have to consider how long you'll be studying for. Of course, there are tuition costs, program fees, and books, but there are also living expenses while studying. Can you afford to move out of your family home and go away to school? You also need a budget for everyday life: food, living expenses, and transportation costs.

You may need to speak to your family or others to really understand the financial impacts of going to school. Talk about what is feasible. Consider whether going to school nearby is a possibility to reduce expenses. If you do consider moving away, determine the time and costs of any travel required and how often you foresee that happening.

Budgeting

When paying for your education, you want to ensure you are prepared. Budgeting and expense tracking are powerful tools because they keep you informed about your money flow and help you develop expertise on financial matters.

Budgets can be done on paper, using an Excel spreadsheet, or on specialty software. The key is to think of the categories that you want to include that capture your income sources and your expenses. The first step is to determine your sources of income such as scholarships, federal, provincial, and territorial grants and loans, Registered Education Savings Plan, part-time jobs and help from friends and family.

Income Sources

Scholarships

Once you have decided on a post-secondary school, consider researching and applying for scholarships. "Every year millions of dollars in post-secondary funding goes unused because qualified students don't apply for scholarships," according to Janet MacDonald, CEO of mycampusgps.ca, who has over 10 years of experience in university admissions and scholarship consulting. She suggests that one key to success is to prepare for scholarships in grade 11. The activities you participate in and your marks in grade 11 are often used to make both admission and scholarship decisions in grade 12.[73]

MacDonald states that, "Grade 12 is the BEST opportunity to get scholarships for university. There will never be another time in your life where there are more opportunities and less competition."

Visit www.mycampusgps.ca to find some free resources. If you want additional support, MacDonald offers essay writing workshops and personalized services, including one-to-one strategy sessions and grade 11 or grade 12 prep packages.

Another source for finding out about scholarships is to visit www.ScholarshipsCanada.com. This company has been helping students find scholarships since 1997 and lists all relevant scholarships and bursaries, free of charge. When students create a free account, they are matched to scholarships and bursaries, and the platform provides additional resources—such as scholarship deadline alerts.[74]

Federal, Provincial, and Territorial Grants and Loans

The Government of Canada, the provinces, and the territories offer student grants and loans. You typically apply for grants and loans in one place within the province of your residence. Loans have to be repaid with interest but grants do not have to be repaid. The amount is determined by a number of factors including your family income, your tuition fees, and living expenses.[75]

Registered Education Savings Plan (RESP)

Some families are able to save for their student's education using an RESP. The RESP is a Canadian government program that combines both saving for a child's education where you can defer the tax on the investment growth and receive direct government grants. Under the Canada Education Savings Grant, the government matches on the first $2,500 contributed annually to the RESP a maximum of $500 per beneficiary, up to a lifetime maximum per beneficiary of $7,200.[76] More details on RESPs can be found at financial institutions such as banks and credit unions.

HigherEdPoints.com

An innovative way to pay for part of your education has been developed by Suzanne Tyson, founder of HigherEdPoints.com. This platform allows students and grads to use anyone's credit card loyalty points to fund tuition and or repay student loans. Loyalty points from Aeroplan, TD Rewards and CIBC can be converted, and additional loyalty partners are in the works.[77]

Instead of redeeming loyalty points for a flight or merchandise, your parents, grandparents, and anyone else can redeem for the HigherEdPoints reward. Through a free HigherEdPoints member account, the funds are deposited directly into your student account at your school or into your Canada Student Loan account.

There is no limit to the amount that can be converted, and students at all stages and ages can use the program—including mature, part-time, and international students.

There are 150 participating institutions[78] from across Canada. Just check HigherEdPoints.com to confirm your institution is on the list. Participating schools include: University of Toronto, McMaster University, University of Waterloo and Brock University. In British Columbia, schools include: Emily Carr University of Art and Design, Capilano University, British Columbia Institute of Technology, Thompson Rivers University, and Vancouver Island University.

Tracking Expenses and Creating a Budget

Next, determine the categories to track your future spending. Consider both one-time expenses and ongoing expenses.

One-time Expenses
- Tuition
- Books
- Computer/laptop

Ongoing Expenses
- Housing
- Cell phone

- WiFi
- Food
  - Groceries
  - Meal plan
  - Snacks/Coffee/Tea
- Rent or residence fees
- Utilities
  - Hydro
  - Heat

Transportation

- Transit
- Parking
- Gas
- Car payments/insurance/maintenance

Travel

- Holidays
- Travel back home

Medical expense

- Prescriptions
- Medical and dental procedures

Clothing

Personal care

Entertainment

Miscellaneous

- Recreation memberships
- Laundry
- Gifts

By calculating both your one-time and ongoing expenses, you can use this information to determine your monthly budget. Some excellent information on budgeting can be found at the Government of Canada website from the Financial Consumer Agency: www.canada.ca/en/financial-consumer-agency/services/ budget-student-life/student-budget-worksheet.html.[79]

A quick and convenient way to calculate your budget is to enter the information into a budget calculator, offered by banks and credit unions like Coast Capital Savings on their websites.[80]

Selecting What is Right for You

There are a lot of details to capture when you are researching schools and programs. Consider capturing the information in a table to help you compare your schools of interest.

Step 16: Considerations: School, Program, & Financial Comparison Table

Customize your own list of considerations. Here is a table to get you started.

Considerations	School A	School B	School C
School Considerations			
School size			
Location of school			
Distance to travel home			
School reputation/rankings			
Extracurricular opportunities: clubs, sports, societies			
Gym/Fitness Centre			

Diversity of student body			
Friends attending			
Program Considerations			
Program admission requirements			
Program application date			
Entrance requirement average			
Program length			
Courses to be taken			
Average class size			
Program prepares me for a future career			
Co-op opportunities are available			
Career Centre services available			
Volunteer opportunities			
International student exchange program			
Financial Considerations			
Cost of tuition			
Cost of books			
Living costs			
Costs to travel home			
Scholarships/bursaries available			

Evaluating Schools and Programs

After determining which programs can lead you to a meaningful career, you may have decided to apply to several schools. The next step is waiting for your offers of acceptance. Offers from schools typically arrive in the spring. The question is, how do you decide which school to go to? Go back to your Considerations Comparison Table and review your notes to help you make your decision.

Overall, you are looking for the best fit for you.

You Can Always Pivot

When you make your decision on which school and program you want, remember that you are basing your decision on the self-knowledge, reflections, and labour market research that you have conducted. You also have had your *ikigai* diagram as a guide or touchstone.

However, as you build your skills, knowledge and learn more about yourself, you can and should update and adapt your *ikigai* diagram with your new information. And this might mean a pivot.

It is to be expected that when you start taking courses at school, you might find there are some courses that you really love and excel at. And, there might be some courses that you don't find interesting. Knowing both what you like and don't like is valuable information and provides you with additional data to tweak or amend your *ikigai* diagram. This is a life-long process!

Summary

In this chapter, "What Education Do You Need?", you researched and prepared a list of schools and programs that will prepare you for careers that you are interested in. You also found out when and how to apply to your programs of interest and prepared a table capturing the information you collected.

One important factor mentioned is cost. This may require opening up the discussion with your loved ones about how you will pay for your education. You may have savings from a part-time job you can contribute to cover costs. Or you might be able to apply for scholarships, bursaries, grants and loans. Perhaps you have a Registered Education Saving Plan (RESP) or financial support from your family. Family and friends can even help pay for your education by contributing their loyalty points to fund your tuition through HigherEdPoints.

Once you accept your offer, you will be on your way, studying to gain new knowledge for your future career.

Moving to the Build Phase

While you are studying, you are building your skills and knowledge. But you can also build your practical experience and your industry connections at the same time. Building your experience and your network *while studying* versus waiting until you graduate will improve your success of landing a meaningful career.

We are now moving into Phase 2: Build, and in the next chapters, we'll discuss proven strategies for improving your chances of finding a meaningful job after graduation. Having taught over 4,000 students, I have seen what works and will share student success stories demonstrating that these are proven principles!

Checklist

- ☐ Online Research: Finding the right program and school
  - ☐ www.workbc.ca
  - ☐ www.schoolfinder.com
- ☐ Paying for your education
- ☐ Income Sources
  - ☐ Scholarships
  - ☐ Federal and Provincial Grants and Loans
  - ☐ HigherEdPoints
  - ☐ RESP
- ☐ Budgeting for Expenses
- ☐ Evaluate using your Considerations: School, Program and Financial Comparison Table

DISCOVER

Before we move into Phase 2: Build, let's recap Phase 1: Discover.

Your *ikigai* Circles

In chapters one, two and three, you worked on several exercises to uncover "What You Are Good At", "What You Love", and "What the World Needs". Based on this, you uncovered the information you needed for filling out circles one, two and three on your *ikigai* diagram. You also created your Personal Mission Statement.

Remember, to ensure that you are working towards a career that will allow you to be financially independent, circles one, two, and three on the *ikigai* diagram should intersect with the fourth circle, called "What You Can be Paid For".

Delving into Careers To Research

In chapter four, you prepared a Career Exploration Plan listing careers to investigate. Then you conducted research to see which careers seemed like a fit, would be in demand, and would allow you financial independence. You were introduced to three ways of finding out more about your list of careers. These three ways were: conduct research on the internet, conduct Informational Interviews, and connect to industry associations. Based on your research, you may have eliminated some careers from your list and now have fewer to move ahead with.

Let's take the time to fill out your *ikigai* diagram located at the back of this book with the information that you have learned so far. Remember, your *ikigai* diagram is dynamic and will evolve as you experience more on your journey, so expect to amend or adapt it.

- **What You Love: Add what you love and your value words**

- **What You Are Good At: Include your strengths and qualities**

- **What the World Needs: Add what you want to see more of in the world**

- **What You Can be Paid For: Write down potential careers of interest**

Training and Education

While exploring careers, you most likely found out that additional knowledge, skills, and certifications were required for the careers you investigated. Online research is one way to identify the schools and programs that offer the training you require and this was covered in chapter five.

Choosing Which School To Say Yes To

It is exciting when you receive an acceptance letter into a program and school. The next challenge is to select, accept, and enroll in a program. There are many factors to consider that will inform which school to select. To help with this decision, you captured information on the schools and their programs in a table for easy review and comparison.

What's Up Next—Phase 2: Build

Once you decide where to study, you will begin the next part of your journey, the Build Phase. This phase includes building your experience, network, and profile, and will be covered in chapters six, seven, and eight.

PHASE 2
BUILD

CHAPTER 6

Build Your Experience

Y ou have made it! You are now enrolled in a program, gaining new knowledge and skills. You are focussed on getting used to this stage of your journey. You are meeting new people and discovering how to master your studies. This all takes some adjusting and that is quite normal. Focussing on your studies is key. However, this is only part of your education. Employers will be looking for grads that have both learned the theory and have some experience in the practical skills required. Therefore, be on the hunt for opportunities where you can build your real-world skills *while you are studying*.

Following, I will share research with you that indicates that employers look for employees that have these practical skills:

- Critical thinking
- Work well on a team
- Have strong collaboration abilities
- Ability to solve complex problems

- Have digital fluency
- Have intercultural competencies

Building these practical skills can be accomplished through participating in work-integrated learning opportunities. Work-integrated learning (WIL) integrates your academic studies within a workplace or practice setting. WIL can occur at the course or program level and includes the development of skills related to employability.[81]

You will build your practical skills by participating in the following WIL activities:

- Co-op work terms
- Internships
- Practicums
- Apprenticeships
- Applied projects
- Starting your own business

You can also build practical skills through:

- Participating in case competitions and debates
- Volunteering
- Taking on a side hustle
- Joining a student club
- Studying abroad
- Attending an international field school

Look out for opportunities that encourage you to "apply" the theory you are learning. Seek out experiences that allow you to build your leadership skills and develop your ability to work effectively with culturally-diverse teams. This might include participating in case competitions or debates on campus. The possibilities are endless!

As you participate in these experiences, take note of what you love and what you are good at. These opportunities provide you with new data that may allow you to update, add to, or adapt your *ikigai* diagram.

In this chapter, we'll cover some key ways to gain practical skills and build your experience.

So what are the skills that you should focus on developing?

Let's look at skills forecasted to be in demand.

Skills in Demand

In the RBC, *Bridging the Gap: Solutions Wanted* study, it is projected that after an assessment of 20,000 skills rankings across 300 occupations, that there will be "an increasing demand for foundational skills such as critical thinking, coordination, social perceptiveness, active listening and complex problem solving."[82] In addition, the report states that, "Digital fluency will be essential to all new jobs. This does not mean we need a nation of coders, but a nation that is digitally literate."[83]

An additional research report called, *Preparing Tomorrow's Workforce for the Fourth Industrial Revolution*, produced by Deloitte and the Global Business Coalition for Educators, identifies the skills needed as "workforce readiness, soft skills, technical skills and entrepreneurship."

Workforce readiness includes building the skills that are addressed in this book, including researching, conducting job search activities, resume writing skills, interview skills, networking, and building your experience.

Soft Skills: Working Well With Others

What are soft skills? "Soft skills" is a phrase used to differentiate from more technical, or "hard skills". Soft skills are important and as stated in the Deloitte report previously mentioned, they include skills in: "Communication, critical thinking, creative thinking, collaboration, adaptability, initiative, leadership, social emotional learning, teamwork, self-confidence, empathy, growth mindset, and cultural awareness."[84]

Cultural Awareness

Skills in cultural awareness or intercultural competencies can improve your ability to effectively communicate across cultures. Given the changing diversity in our workplaces and work teams, these skills are needed now more than ever and, in fact, you have likely been building cultural competencies already. Many of you have been in a class made up of students with a variety of back-grounds and worldviews that are different than one another and perhaps your own. Honing your ability to be curious, with an aim to understand others, builds your skill in working with diverse teams in the workplace.

Jaspreet, an international student in my marketing class, pointed this out to me. Jaspreet was part of a class project team with members from Vietnam, India, Brazil and Taiwan. Jaspreet said that working on the group project with his team-mates allowed him to develop his team building skills. He was figuring out how to collaborate with individuals from a variety of cultures that also had different perspectives.

As many organizations operate in the global economy, soft skills such as intercultural competencies are considered very important skills by employers. The RBC *Bridging the Gap* report states that "Global competencies like cultural awareness, language, and adaptability will be in demand."[85]

According to the Deloitte Report *Preparing Tomorrow's Workforce for the Fourth Industrial Revolution,* the future workplace will require technical and "soft skills in cross-cultural, multicultural, and global contexts". These global and intercultural competencies are the skills associated with intercultural communication and intercultural development and are seen as extremely valuable. Sent to employers and students on behalf of the Association of American Colleges and Universities, a 2015 survey by Hart Associates reported that nearly all employers surveyed (96%) agreed that "all college students should have experiences that teach them how to solve problems with people whose views are different from their own."[86]

The ability to notice and understand cultural differences and then know how to accomplish shared goals are sought-after skills in our global world.

These are skills that are important for all students, whether you grew up in Canada or are a newcomer to the country. Students from international pathways have the opportunity to highlight to Canadian employers that they bring an additional and valuable worldview to the workplace. Remember that your international perspective is something to showcase and celebrate.

So we have an idea now of the many skills that employers are looking for. You can gain these practical skills by participating in a variety of experiences, all *while you are studying.* In my teaching, I have observed many students successfully embrace opportunities to build their experience and have seen how these experiences provide them with real-time data, informing their path to a meaningful career.

Cooperative Education or Co-op Work Terms

Many colleges and universities have programs that allow you to alternate terms of study with paid work or co-op terms. Typically, the length of a co-op work term is the same as one semester, or it can span two or three semesters. Most post-secondary institutions have a Co-op and Career Education Centre where you can find out more about the co-op option. Most likely the programs that will have co-op work terms are Business, Computer Science, Engineering, and Sciences. Note, you may need to apply separately to be able to participate in the Cooperative Education program, so be sure to research this well.

Co-op and Career Centres typically offer resume writing and interview skill preparation workshops for you to take advantage of. Co-op work terms are great opportunities to build your critical thinking and soft skills. In addition, you can work for an organization or industry that you are interested in. During my Master's degree, I completed three co-op work terms in the marketing field and these experiences allowed me to find out about different roles, different employers, and whether I was a fit for the organizations I worked at.

You never know what you will learn from your work terms. After I completed three work terms, one of my main takeaways was finding the preferred "size" of company I wanted to work for when I graduated.

Goldilocks and the Three Bears

Finding out which size of company I preferred was a little like the story of Goldilocks and the Three Bears. I had my first work term at the Canadian Imperial Bank of Commerce (CIBC) and this company had 3500 employees, all located in one office tower. That firm was too big for me.

My second work term was at an employer that had 15 employees. That firm was too small for me. It was during my third work term at an office with 200 employees where I realized that the size of that firm felt just right. When I graduated, I ended up seeking employment at another firm that had 200 employees. During my interview, I confirmed that the size of the firm felt like a good fit based on what I had learned on my work terms.

What other benefit can be gained by completing a co-op work term? While you can't always predict, it might lead to a full-time job!

Argi's Success Story:
Making Connections at the Highest Level

Argi, a marketing management student, was interested in a career in event marketing, having really enjoyed her event marketing course. She also liked working with people. Her school's Co-op Officer presented her with a co-op opportunity to apply for at a large non-profit called the United Way as a Campaign Associate. This role involved event marketing. She applied for the role and was accepted for a four-month paid co-op work term. Argi was assigned to connect and support accounts that were in government and at post-secondary institutions in the Lower Mainland.

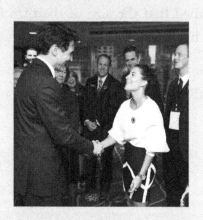

It was here that Argi was able to build on her ability to make connections and support the many fundraising events that were happening at her accounts. It also gave her great experience working with senior executives including the Mayor of Vancouver. During this work term, she gained a set of skills that she was able to leverage to secure a role at the Greater Vancouver Board of Trade upon graduating—a role that included her love of events, connecting with people, and working with senior executives. That is, if you call Prime Minister Justin Trudeau and Barack Obama senior executives!

Source: Matt Borck, Argi Ahmadi and Prime Minister Justin Trudeau, 2018, photograph, Vancouver, British Columbia.

Internships

Internships are another way to build your experience and leadership skills while at school.

A local credit union in British Columbia has offered students in grades 11 and 12 an opportunity to be part of their Youth Intern Program. It is a one-year paid internship and the interns work at the credit union's branches as member service representatives and as community ambassadors at local events. These roles allow students to obtain skills in leadership, community relations, and financial literacy. It has been a full-time role in the summer and part-time role on the weekend during the school year.[87]

Some internships are paid and some are unpaid. Some high schools and post-secondary institutions offer students academic credits as part of the internship experience. Internships allow students to work with local organizations and build their experience.

While it may not make sense for some people, there are firms that take on students on an unpaid basis, and the internships are not officially part of an education program. Most companies are moving away from this option preferring to pay students or be part of an official program where students earn credits at their institution.

However, it might be a fit for you to pursue an unpaid internship when you consider the potential benefits. For instance, you might complete an internship and quickly pick up valuable public relations skills. That is what Trevor did.

Trevor's Success Story:
Picking Up Skills a Few Hours a Week

Trevor, a marketing student, was interested in a public relations career but felt like he didn't have enough work experience in this area. During one of his marketing classes, a guest speaker from a small media agency came to speak. After the speaker was finished, Trevor introduced himself and followed up. He arranged a coffee meeting with the speaker and shared that he was looking for experience. The agency brought Trevor on as an unpaid public relations intern for several hours a week. Trevor then leveraged this experience to obtain a full-time communications and public relations role at an upcoming and growing company after he graduated. Trevor has continued to build on his communications skills and currently works for a botanical and essence company leading their marketing communications, merging his passion for wellness with the skills he is good at.

Student Clubs

A great way to build experience, flex your leadership skills, and stand out from the crowd is to volunteer or even start your own student club or society. High schools and post-secondary institutions have a variety of clubs and often hold "Clubs and Societies Day" so you can see the clubs you might want to join. Fulvia and Flavia revived a club that complemented the marketing subject they were studying.

Fulvia's and Flavia's Success Story: Taking the Lead to Get Ahead

Fulvia and Flavia were in the Post-Degree Diploma in Marketing Management program. They were invited by their instructor to attend an industry advisory meeting for the Marketing Management Department. At this meeting, they heard straight from employers about the exact skills they were looking for from marketing grads. This was exciting information and was going to bring changes in the marketing management program such as adding certifications in Google Ad Words and Hootsuite. However, these changes were not going to be implemented until after Fulvia and Flavia had graduated from the program!

Now, the young women had heard about a club that operated at the college called the Digital Media Marketing Club. However, the club had closed down the year before as no one had taken over its leadership. Fulvia and Flavia decided to bring the club back to life, and as executives of the club, recruited student members. They approached and contacted industry executives to come speak at club member meetings, building their professional network. They also organized workshops so their club members could complete the "in-demand" certifications in Google Ad Words and Hootsuite. By volunteering to run the club, these two students gained leadership experience and improved their digital media marketing skills, setting them apart from the crowd.

What if you can't find a student club that you are interested in volunteering at? Consider starting your own club. That is exactly what Martina did.

Martina's Success Story:
Creating Something Brand New

Martina, a marketing student, was really interested in both fashion and digital media. She formed her own club and as president of the club, she was able to set the direction on what events and activities the club focussed on. She created opportunities to build her leadership skills in an industry she was passionate about.

Side Hustles

Paid work allows you to gain experience and skills, and can help you stand out from the crowd. One way to demonstrate your ingenuity is to develop a "side hustle" or secure some gig-work. In the report, *Preparing Tomorrow's Workforce* it states that "late in the 2000s we saw the rise of the gig economy." The gig economy might include work that supplements full-time work with gig-work—also called side hustles. Or sometimes people have more than one gig job that adds up to full-time employment.[88] The 2020 pandemic has fueled this trend of gig and contract work.

Seventy-three percent of students will need a job to have enough money to go to school, according to a survey with over 10,000 Canadian and International students surveyed in August 2020 by Customer Relationship Index Inc. (cri) and the SchoolFinder Group.[89]

James Lau, Founder of Apologue, has a great list of gig and side-hustle ideas. James founded his company to help young people identify their purpose and accelerate their growth so that they can live a more fulfilling life. He offers coaching and mentoring and some great tips on how to fund your education while building skills that will help you stand out.

James outlines in his blog article "15 Side Hustles to Start in University" ideas such as tutoring, freelancing on sites like Fiverr and Upworks, using your car to drive for Uber or delivering food through DoorDash, charging for proofreading services, providing your photography services to student clubs, starting a YouTube channel, and many other ideas. To learn more about Apologue and to request a copy of the article "15 Side Hustles to Start in University" go to www.apologue.net/contact/.[90] While helping fund your education, these side hustles allow you to develop your problem-solving skills and demonstrate your initiative.

Side Hustle Ideas

- Tutoring other students
- Freelancing on Fiverr and Upworks
- Driving for Uber, DoorDash, UberEats
- Writing and posting on Medium under their partner program
- Forming your own social media agency
- Proofreading
- Photography
- Starting a YouTube channel
- Creating a course [91]

Project-Based Learning

More and more instructors are adding applied learning opportunities into their classes by inserting realistic class projects encouraging you to partner with real companies. This project-based learning provides you with a few unique opportunities to leverage.

First, if the instructor allows you to choose the organization to partner with, I suggest you think of an organization in the industry you are interested in working in and target that firm. Contacting a company with an idea for a school project provides you with a unique opening. You have a legitimate reason to reach out to key people that you are interested in meeting.

If you are passionate about a career in sports marketing, perhaps you can work on a project for a local sports team. Or if you are interested in working on addressing youth mental health issues, you could contact a non-profit organization working on this issue. Tying the project to what you want to change in the world will make the project more meaningful to you.

Working with real organizations allows you to acquire in-depth knowledge of the sector, build up experience, and make valuable connections. Ideally, these connections will continue on after your school project is completed. It is the industry connections that you have made that can provide you with job referrals and all sorts of opportunities. During my years of teaching, I have seen many students benefit from these connections, leading them to full-time job opportunities. This happened to Rodrigo.

Rodrigo's Success Story:
Car Theft Opens Doors

Rodrigo, an international student from Brazil, was completing his post-degree diploma and had just arrived in Canada with years of marketing and brand management experience working at major firms in his home country. What he needed was contacts in his new country, and, as a married man with children, he wanted to secure employment quickly. In his marketing course, he worked on an applied marketing project with a real client, the Royal Canadian Mounted Police (RCMP). The students were asked to develop an advertising and social media campaign aimed at reducing car thefts and increasing awareness in the public on how to prevent their cars from being stolen.

The groups presented their campaigns to the RCMP client. The RCMP officer was very impressed with the presentations and the organization decided that they would hire someone to implement the social media campaign ideas. The role was posted as a four-month work term and Rodrigo applied and was hired! Later the role was extended and Rodrigo stayed on for eight more months, all as a result of completing an in-class applied project and developing the connection.

Volunteering

If you don't have a lot of paid work experience, then spending your time volunteering can help you gain experience, skills, and knowledge. Keep an eye out for volunteer roles promoted to you by your instructors or professors.

Volunteer on Campus

Your campus or high school may post volunteer opportunities

that allow you to build skills that are needed for your future career, all while you are studying. This is important and will help you stand out to employers when looking for a job.

It is important to note that details from your volunteer experience can be shared in an interview, demonstrating what you have learned. You can share how you successfully led a team or built new competencies. Nick was a student that volunteered and was able to build his digital fluency.

Nick's Success Story:
Volunteering to Build Social Media Skills

Nick, a marketing student, was looking to gain hands-on social media experience. A volunteer opportunity came up to become a social media ambassador for the faculty department he was in. He was responsible for creating, posting, and evaluating daily content on Facebook. This allowed him to add the duties and the title of "Social Media Ambassador" to his resume and his LinkedIn profile. Nick was able to pick up applied experience, building his resume while completing his marketing degree.

Volunteer with Industry Associations

Volunteering for a role within an industry association is a way to accelerate connecting with industry professionals you wish to work with.

You can develop new skills while you work alongside industry professionals and they get to "see you in action" on committees. You build your network and profile in the industry in a way that even a paid job might not provide. You are able to bring your skills to the role. Christian did just that. He volunteered with an industry association, bringing his fantastic people skills and organizational abilities.

Christian's Success Story: First Step to Presidency

Christian had just completed his Bachelor of Business Administration degree and wanted to build up his experience. It just so happened that I had recently accepted a role on an industry association's Board of Directors as the Director of Sponsorship. I was looking for a graduated student to help me grow the sponsorship portfolio of clients.

I asked Christian to volunteer in the role, knowing he had excellent people skills. Also, the volunteer opportunity would provide him with access to contacts in the marketing industry. Christian accepted and excelled in the role where he supported the sponsors. When I stepped down, Christian stepped up to replace me as Director of Sponsorship. He continued to grow in his experience and responsibility and he eventually became the President of the BC Chapter of the American Marketing Association. He is now well-known and connected in the local marketing community as a result.

International Field Schools

If you have travelled to other countries, you will know that there is something very transformational about travelling to another place. Living in another country and studying there will provide you with insights into different cultures and ways of thinking about the world as you experience it first-hand. Some high schools and most post-secondary institutions offer international opportunities such as International Field Schools and study abroad opportunities.

Canadian students don't travel to study as much as students in other countries. In the *Canadian International Strategy Document for 2010-2024* it refers to the report by the Study Group on Global Education that estimates that "approximately 11% of Canadian undergraduates study abroad during their academic career—significantly fewer than students from France (33%), Australia (19%) and the United States (16%).[92]

Travelling and studying abroad will help you improve your intercultural competency skills.

Look for opportunities to study abroad, travel, or seek out courses that will provide you with language skills or insights into other cultures and their perspectives. If you are already in college or university, consider taking courses like, "Introduction to Latin Studies" or "Introduction to Asian Studies" to broaden your outlook.

International Field Schools are offered to students and consist of a two or three-week international trip accompanied by one or two instructors. Students are awarded credits for completing the trip and are perhaps required to complete some additional coursework. These trips provide amazing chances to experience new cultures and experience what it might be like to live there. You will be exposed to different cultural value systems that might challenge your own perspectives.

Study Abroad

Some schools offer programs that allow you to study at international partner schools. This might be just for one term or even for one year. These international institutional partnerships are often already set up by your home school and there might be additional support for you provided by your home school when you study with an international partner. You might receive help with arranging accommodation, advice on course selection, and sometimes even be assigned a local student buddy to help you settle in when you arrive. Kayli was very interested in studying abroad and wanted to experience a new culture.

**Kayli's Success Story:
So Many Places to Go!**

Kayli, a graphic design student, loved design and wanted to travel. Her four-year Bachelor of Design program provided an opportunity to study abroad at a choice of partner schools in Europe, Australia, and many other places. The timing was limited to only studying in the second semester of her second year. Supported by the International Study Abroad Department at her university, she was able to investigate the programs online and narrowed her choices down to studying in either Amsterdam or Barcelona.

Obtaining international experience helps you to understand other cultures and gain insights into cultural differences in communication, teamwork, and decision making. These are highly valued skills that employers are looking for, especially as the workforce of today is increasingly becoming more diverse and requires intercultural competencies.

And for those students from international pathways studying in Canada, please recognize that you bring unique and valuable global perspectives to any workplace you apply to!

Online International Learning Opportunities

Can't travel? Schools are now developing online international partnerships that allow students to build their intercultural skills. Many schools are offering Collaborating Online International Learning (COIL) opportunities where students work on projects together with students at international schools. COIL programs use technology to bridge the distance, allowing students to connect with those from different cultures, work together on initiatives, and build global understanding.

So how will you build your experience? Review the ways to build your practical skills in the table in Step 1 and set some goals to find out more.

Step 1: Outline the Activities to Pursue to Build Your Experience and Practical Skills

Build your Experience	Details	Contact Info	Date to complete by
Find out about co-op and internship opportunities			
List some side hustles to explore			

Identify possible volunteer opportunities			
Possible clubs to join			
List International Field Schools			
List study abroad opportunities			

Summary

This chapter has been focussed on the many ways you can build your experience and gain in-demand skills, all *while you are studying*. Consider participating in co-op work terms, internships, side hustles, volunteering, joining or even starting your own club to build your soft skills. Or consider participating in an International Field School or a study abroad term to learn about other cultures. All of these experiences will help you build the skills that employers are looking for—skills in collaboration, communication, teamwork, critical thinking, and cultural awareness.

The most successful students focus on their studies AND dedicate time to building and developing their practical skills. Students that don't allocate time to building their experience while studying will be at a disadvantage once they graduate.

In the next chapter, "Build Your Network", we'll talk about building your professional network *while you are studying* so that before you graduate, you will be connected to those that can hire you when you've finished your studies.

Checklist

☐ Contact the Co-op and Career Centre on your campus to find out about co-op opportunities

☐ Determine which campus clubs or societies you can join, or start your own club to build your leadership skills

☐ Investigate a new side hustle to develop new skills

☐ Seek out volunteer opportunities on campus

☐ Participate in International Field Schools and/or study abroad to build your intercultural competencies

CHAPTER 7

Build Your Network

During Phase 2: Build, the focus is on building your experience, your network, and your profile. The previous chapter focused on tips for building your experience and practical skills through a variety of ways such as participating in co-op work terms or internships, starting a side hustle, volunteering on campus, or through a school club. The goal is to seek out opportunities where you can develop the in-demand skills that employers look for. These are all ways to build your **experience,** *while you are studying.*

In this chapter, I want to share ways you can build your **network,** also *while you are studying.*

When you build your network, you make industry connections. As you speak with these connections, you will find out about the careers, companies, and industries you are exploring. This new information might cause you to update, add, or adapt your *ikigai* diagram.

This chapter builds on the career exploration skills you developed previously. Recall that in chapter four, you were asked to conduct online research, arrange informational interviews, and connect to industry associations. Connecting to industry professionals allows employers to get to know you while you are a student. As a result, you may hear about employment opportunities first-hand because these industry connections are plugged in to the job market. They are part of a network that communicates information about newly posted jobs. They share intel on which companies are hiring and which companies are great to work for.

Wouldn't it be nice being the first to hear about newly-posted jobs? In addition, industry professionals are often aware of job opportunities that are in the *hidden job market*. These job opportunities may never be posted as they are filled through referrals and connections. So how do you connect to industry players that know about *newly posted* positions? How do you access the *hidden job market?*

You need to build your network. And it is not as hard as you think. First, let's begin with who you already know.

Connect to Family and Friends

Start with your own family. Who do you know? Where do they work? Now think of the friends that you know. Then think of their families. Where do they work? Don't forget that your family and the family of your friends, all work in a variety of careers. Your family and your friends are people that know you well. They are great people to chat with about their careers. Ask them what they like about their careers and what they don't like. They want to help you. They have seen you grow up and take on new responsibilities. Don't be surprised to find out that these strong ties are really interested in helping you succeed and are open to referring you to others in their network or being a personal reference.

Kyle's Success Story:
Value in Your Strong Ties

Kyle has been friends with Sasha since he was five years old and they knew each other well. Over the years, Sasha's parents also got to know Kyle, his interests, and his personality. Sasha's parents worked in education, just like his own parents.

When Kyle was in grade 11, guess who became the principal of Kyle's high school? Yes, Sasha's dad, Dr. Schofield. When Kyle was in grade 12 applying for university, he was required to submit references and needed to ask someone that knew him well enough to write a reference letter for him. He realized, who better to ask than someone who had known him since he was five years old, was the principal of his high school, and could speak to his abilities as a high school student.

It is well documented that weak ties can also be beneficial, according to Mark S Granovetter, author of "The Strength of Weak Ties". Weak ties are connections to those just outside of your friends and family. Granovetter suggests those that move in different circles from our own have access to information different from what we can access.[93] So keep that in mind when someone offers to connect you to their cousin that knows a friend of a friend that works at the company you are interested in!

Family and Friends Want to Help

Family friends can provide you with the valuable insight they have gained from their experiences. When I was in my third year of undergraduate studies in psychology, I abruptly realized that the psychology degree I was completing was not going to lead directly to a career. I was very shocked and disappointed. I felt I had been misled! However, it was the son of my parents' friends that really helped me see a new path forward and it happened in an unusual way. My dad invited me to join him, the family friend and her son who was a bit older than me, for lunch.

At first, I wasn't sure if my father was setting me up on a date! But by dessert it all became clear. The son had just completed his MBA and he was going to tell me about the program. I had never heard of an MBA which stands for Master of Business Administration. I listened and thought about it and it seemed to line up with what I was naturally good at. I had discovered while working at a publishing company during the summer as a customer service representative that I enjoyed business—the role allowed me to use my communication and organizational skills. I decided to look into the program and I ended up applying for it.

Now it's your turn, add to your Informational Interview Contact Plan started in chapter four.

Step 2: Update Informational Interview Contact Plan

List the careers you are interested in and the names of people you know that are working in careers of interest. Find out their contact information and add this to the chart.

Career	Name	Contact Info

Connect with Instructors

While each educational program is different, your instructors are often well-connected.

Instructors have industry experience and are required to stay up-to-date on new developments in their fields. This means going to events, conducting research, and staying in touch with industry professionals and employers. In fact, employers see instructors as a resource. I am often asked by employers to promote job openings to my students.

Introduce yourself to your instructors. If you have the opportunity, ask if you can connect with them on LinkedIn. Once connected on LinkedIn, you can follow their posts and see who your instructors are connected to. Many of my former students follow me on LinkedIn. I share many association event notifications and job postings. Actually, you never know where the next opportunity might magically appear that is a perfect fit for you! This happened to one of my students Kaely, a student with a love for film arts and who was good at marketing.

Kaely's Success Story:
Staying Connected Pays Off

Kaely and I were connected on LinkedIn and she saw a post that I shared promoting an opening for a marketing role at a local film school. She had already completed her Bachelor in Business Administration degree in Marketing Management. When she saw my post, she thought it was a perfect role for her. It fit her interest in film and her experience in event marketing. She applied and got the job!

Connect with Professionals on Campus

Keep an eye out for chances to connect with employers that come to campus to recruit, speak at career panels, or guest speak in your class. Employers that come on campus understand that students gain a lot hearing from people working in different careers. These individuals are open to connecting with you and may be looking for candidates to hire—at that time or in the future.

So don't be shy and do take the opportunity to approach them. Thank the guest speaker after class. Make sure to introduce yourself to make a personal connection. Follow up via email or connect with them on LinkedIn. You never know where these opportunities will lead.

Michael's Success Story:
Networking While in Class

Michael was a student looking to gain marketing experience. A guest speaker from a marketing agency came to his class. The speaker was also on the lookout for a marketing student to fill a co-op work term at his firm. Michael was very engaged during the presentation, asking questions and followed up with the speaker after class. Michael applied for the co-op work term role and was hired by the guest speaker he had first met while in class. After Michael finished that work term, he continued to build on the marketing experience he had gained and has transitioned into a successful career in marketing, post-graduation.

Connect with Alumni

Your college or university wants to see you succeed and often they will host events to facilitate building your network while you are still at school. Schools hold alumni and student networking events to connect alumni that are working in the careers that students want to explore.

Look out for events like the one at my college called "The Networking Essentials Event". This event is held for alumni and students providing them with network opportunities. Students get to practice their networking skills with alumni at the event. The alumni volunteer to attend the event as a way to give back to students. Meanwhile, the alumni connect and continue to build their own network with the other alumni.

It is important to know that once you graduate, you become a member of a huge network of people that continue to support each other, long after you have finished your studies.

Priscilla's and Michelle's Success Story: Helping Each Other Out

A former student of mine, Michelle, contacted me to say she was moving back to Canada from England. She had found a role that she was interested in at TELUS, a telecommunications company. Michelle wanted to find out more about the company and asked if I had any contacts working there. Priscilla came to mind, who was also a graduate of the college where I work and was working at TELUS.

I reached out to see if Priscilla would be open to an Informational Interview with Michelle and she was. I connected the two of them, with Priscilla kindly providing Michelle with insights on the company and the culture. This helped Michelle prepare for her interview ... which must have gone well as she received an offer from TELUS!

Connect to Alumni through Ten Thousand Coffees

Some institutions like Fanshawe College have partnered with Ten Thousand Coffees, a digital platform that matches alumni and students so they can meet for coffee.[94] Find out if your post-secondary institution has partnered with this platform so you can participate, too.

Here is advice from the CEO of Ten Thousand Coffees, Dave Wilkin, from his article in the *Globe and Mail*. He simplifies it this way, "Networking doesn't have to be intimidating, my advice is to just go have a conversation. Maybe you'll help someone; maybe they'll help you. Maybe all you did was practice meeting new people. Perhaps you made a great new connection. In all those scenarios, you'll develop and you'll learn. Either way, you win."[95]

Connect with Mentors

Have you heard of mentorship? Mentorship is when some-one with some life experience—the mentor—provides guidance to another person, called the mentee.

Mentorship can be formal or informal. You might already have mentors that are interested in your career development that you call when you need some advice or want to bounce ideas around. It might be a family member, teacher, or coach that you reach out to.

It is important to have mentors provide feedback so you can get out of your own bubble and see a different perspective. Is there someone that comes to mind that you could consider as a mentor? You can also be a mentor to others, for example, to your younger siblings.

Formal Mentorship

There are some formal mentorship programs out there, like the Greater Vancouver Board of Trade, Leaders of Tomorrow Program.[96] This program has been around since 1999 and is a program that "connects post-secondary students with leading industry professionals."

This program matches mentees with mentors that are working in industry. The mentors provide the mentees with guidance, advice, and sometimes connections in the mentee's desired field of work.

The program encourages volunteerism, providing students opportunities for volunteering on board committees alongside working professionals. In addition, the program hosts networking events so students can connect with business leaders. Sometimes after the networking events, students in the program are allowed to meet with the speakers in small question-and-answer sessions. Hundreds of students have participated in this program, to accelerate their leadership abilities, and build their professional network.

Informal Mentorship

Informal mentors are people that you meet that can provide tips, tricks, advice, and connections but are not formally in a "mentorship" role. For instance, Michelle was a student that participated in the Leaders of Tomorrow program and did have a formal mentor. However, she also had access to me, her former instructor, as an informal mentor.

Michelle's Success Story: Mentors See Things You Don't

When Michelle joined the Red Academy organization, her initial role was as the Admissions Assistant. After meeting with her for a coffee, we discussed how she could expand her role based on the skills and knowledge she had gained while completing her marketing management degree.

Michelle approached the company's senior manager and requested if she could add additional tasks to her duties such as event marketing and promotions.

Her manager agreed and Michelle was able to grow in her role. She was eventually promoted to open up an office in London, England.

Connect with Professionals at Association Events

Every industry you are interested in working in has an association. These associations usually require working professionals to pay for a membership to join but the associations are often open to having students and non-members attend their events. Remember, some associations offer lower-priced student membership or provide volunteer opportunities so that students can attend events for free.

Association events serve as a quick way to network, volunteer, and make connections with people currently working in the field. These associations are often open to having students attend and volunteer at their events and their members are interested in meeting students.

Attending events, whether in person or virtually, offers you the chance to connect and hear about "best practices" from industry professionals. Members of industry associations might have newly started their career or might be people in their mid-careers or senior executives.

Events are a unique way to understand what an industry sector is all about and could provide information allowing you update, add to, or adapt your *ikigai* diagram.

Industry associations might also be a source of information on salary ranges so you can add to circle four, "What You Can be Paid For". And through connecting with others, you can uncover the type of knowledge and skills required to be successful and see if that matches with your own unique strengths or "What You Are Good At". This is exactly what happened to Ryan.

Ryan's Success Story: Flexing His Talents

Ryan attended a BC Chapter of the Association of Integrated Marketers event as part of his marketing course, with his classmates and with me his instructor. At the end of the session, he came running over to me excited and in disbelief. He shared with me that he had just been asked to run a workshop for the industry professional he had sat next to!

Ryan explained that he was sketching out some social media concepts on a napkin for the executive sitting next to him when he asked Ryan if he could come and explain those concepts to his team!

Ryan found an opportunity to share what he was naturally good at.

Tips for Attending a Networking Event

If you recall, in chapter four we covered how connecting to an association of industry professionals is a useful way to explore if a sector is a fit for you. Visiting an association's website provides information on past and upcoming networking events. If you sign up for their newsletters, you will receive emails with information about future events, activities, and sometimes job postings. On the website, check the list of upcoming activities, the dates, and prices of event tickets. You might have to pay a non-member rate, or, look to see if there is a student price.

One way you might be able to attend the event for free is to contact the association and ask if they are looking for any volunteers to set up, sit at the registration desk, or take down at the end of the event.

Tip #1 Go with Someone

You might be more comfortable attending an event with someone. That way you are not on your own. Prepare ahead of time—bring some business cards as giving your business card will facilitate receiving someone else's card. This will allow you to follow up later.

If you're attending an in-person event, plan to give yourself extra time to arrive at the event so you can find the venue, park, and find the specific room where the event is held. You don't want to feel rushed and you do want to arrive on time. And rest assured, it is quite normal to feel slightly uncomfortable when you go to a networking event as you may not know how to approach someone.

Here are some tips.

When you arrive, look around and find the registration desk. Here you provide your name and will receive your name tag. You might be there to learn more about the industry you're interested in from the guest speakers and panelists. However, if you are there to network, you will want to connect with people eventually. So how do you go about that?

One tip is choosing a place to sit next to someone that is alone. Or look for a table with someone already sitting at it, where they are on their own. Say hello and ask if the seat by them is available. Most likely, that person will be grateful to have you to talk to!

Introduce yourself and ask them their name. You can get the conversation started by beginning with some general comments about the weather or perhaps a current event that is in the news. This might even be a chance to share your elevator pitch.

Tip #2 Prepare your Elevator Pitch

You may have heard the phrase "elevator pitch". It comes from the concept of having the rare opportunity of being on an elevator with a senior executive or someone you are keen to meet. You have just a couple of minutes to "pitch" your idea to them before the elevator door opens and lets them off at their floor.

Your elevator pitch is a good thing to rehearse before attending a networking event. The elevator pitch is usually 60 seconds long. The goal is to give someone a quick sense of where you are at and what you are interested in.

For instance, a student at a marketing association networking event might say to an executive:

"Hi, my name is Janelle, and I am in the third year of my Bachelor of Administration degree. I am majoring in marketing and I am really interested in digital marketing careers here in Vancouver."

This quickly gives the person an understanding that Janelle is a student that is still in school, which means that she is not available to work full-time yet. They hear from her that she is interested in exploring careers in digital marketing. This information lets the industry professional quickly know where she is at and what she is interested in.

If the executive has expertise in digital marketing, they could discuss this with the student. Or if this is not their field, the executive might refer the student to someone they know that does work in digital marketing. Believe it or not, this happened to Erick.

Erick's Success Story:
It's a Small World

Erick, an international student from England, attended his first Canadian networking event. He had just met an executive, introduced himself, and shared the field he was interested in. The executive immediately said, "I know someone you should speak to. Here's my card, contact me and I will connect you."

Erik told me that his mouth opened wide and he just said to the person next to him, "Did that just happen?"

You might feel like you don't have anything to offer, however, you would be surprised how valuable your insight and skills are to others. The goal is to connect, ask questions, and also—believe it or not—see how you can help the other person. You might be surprised how your experience and knowledge are valued. Remember this was something that surprised Ryan when he attended an industry event.

Tip #3 Follow Up

It is a good idea to follow up after the event with the connections you made. Some people are open to connecting on LinkedIn and if you send a personalized LinkedIn invite after the event, you might be able to connect to them through this platform.

A personalized LinkedIn invite could include referring to when and where you met, and that you would like to link in, if they are interested.

Or a follow up email is also appropriate. Again, remind the person how you met and the details of your conversation so that they can remember you. A simple thank you and a follow-up is typical and depending on the depth of your conversation, consider requesting an Informational Interview in your email.

Here is a sample follow-up email:

> "It was a pleasure to meet you last Friday at the Board of Trade breakfast event. I really enjoyed our conversation. As you know, I am incredibly interested in the field of accounting and would love to hear more about your career journey. Would you have time for a coffee or phone call so I could hear more and ask you about the industry?"

Networking at association events gives you the chance to connect with senior executives that are often busy and hard to reach. Rodolfo leveraged an opportunity to meet the vice president of a company that was on his exploration list, and following up led him to a key step on his career journey.

Rodolfo's Success Story: Gooaaal!

Rodolfo, an international student from Brazil, loved soccer. And when he was completing his post-degree diploma in marketing, he told everyone he met that he would love to work with the Vancouver Whitecaps FC. When an opportunity came up for students to attend a networking event to meet marketing and advertising executives, he jumped at the chance. The speed-mentoring event was put on by the National Advertising Benevolent Society (NABS) which is the association of media/advertising/marketing professionals and Rodolfo's college was sponsoring the event.

This event was designed to provide students the opportunity to connect with at least five advertising/marketing professionals. While students could submit their five preferences, Rodolfo did not receive one of his top selections which was to meet with the VP Marketing of the Whitecaps, the local soccer franchise. But that didn't stop us! In the break, I introduced Rodolfo to the VP of Marketing and then made my exit. Rodolfo continued with the conversation and established a connection, obtained the VP's business card, and was able to secure an Informational Interview a few weeks later.

Nothing resulted immediately. However, six months later, I saw Rodolfo at another event, and he ran over and excitedly shared with me that as a direct result of that introduction to the Whitecaps' VP of Marketing, he was contacted by them and was starting a job there the next Monday—the exact organization he had set his sights on!

Tip #4 Attend the Right Event

A mistake I made? I once went to the wrong event! The joys of networking. Early in my marketing career, I attended BC American Marketing Association (BCAMA) networking events to hear industry speakers, connect, and build my network of marketing professionals.

The events were always in the same venue and began at 5:30 pm. I noted that at the previous events I had attended, the food went quite quickly as everyone was pretty hungry coming straight after work. One time, when I walked into the event, I noticed that the food was quite great this time, lots of large, meaty sandwiches. I grabbed a plate and sat down at a table with other people to begin networking. I introduced myself to a gentleman and I noticed he was wearing a name tag from one of the banks. We began chatting and as I chomped down on my sandwich, I thought it was a curious thing that he was wearing his work name tag. We continued chatting and then all of a sudden, I realized that everyone was wearing a name tag, from the same bank. Yikes! I was in the wrong event and eating their food! So yes, I quickly finished the sandwich and left the room to discover that my event was actually next door to the one I had crashed!

Next, update your list of associations from Chapter 4 adding to the table in Step 3 on the next page and indicate if you will either join, volunteer, attend an event, or sign up for their newsletter.

Step 3: Update your List of Associations and Set Some Goals

Name of Association	Attend an event	Join as a member	Volunteer	Sign up for a newsletter

Happenstance Learning Theory

The definition of happenstance is "something that happens by chance". The Happenstance Learning Theory suggests "that human behaviour is the product of learning experiences made available by both planned and unplanned situations in which individuals find themselves."[97]

What this means is that while we all like to plan, some things in life happen to us that we have no control over, that we didn't plan. Things like who your parents are, where you were born, and what language you speak. However, that does not mean you don't have control over your world. You actually have a great deal of control because you can take actions that might result in unplanned events. In fact, all the exploratory actions you are taking can generate beneficial unplanned events.[98]

You could think of this as creating luck or chances. So how does creating chances play a role in finding your meaningful career? Well, take Ted Robinson for example, a well-known San Francisco Giants broadcaster. When he was asked how he started his career in sports broadcasting, he said, "It was just a fluke."

Ted Robinson described in an interview how he got his first job in the major leagues. He called the Oakland A's office and the thing is … the team owner answered his phone call. Ted began talking and the next thing Ted knew, he had a job interview lined up. A chance event did occur, the owner of the team answered the phone.

However, before this chance event turned lucky for Ted, let me tell you something about him. He had worked as a college broadcaster during his student years (so he had some skills) and he had also researched and knew the team owner of the Oakland A's was open to hiring new, less experienced talent. And Ted took the initiative to make the phone call. He did not know who would answer the call but he placed the call then seized upon the chance to sell his talents. [99]

Planning Happenstance

So another concept we should talk about is planning happenstance. Yes, planning for something to happen by chance! How do you plan to create more chances for good things to happen for you? Here are just a few ways to create chances for the unplanned to happen:

- Take a class directly or remotely connected to an interest of yours
- Contact potential employers to conduct Informational Interviews

- Network at industry events
- Volunteer, intern, or apply for a co-op job
- Talk to the person next to you on the bus!

Volunteering in even a small way might lead to chance opportunities that you would never have known about! One year, I was asked by my college to speak to some senior executives that were visiting from China about the Leaders of Tomorrow Mentorship program. I was presenting along with my industry colleague, the program manager from the Board of Trade. That year, Argi, who we heard about earlier, was my mentee. I asked Argi if she would volunteer to present with me, as I wanted her to share her perspective on the program as a mentee. Little did we know where it would lead.

Argi's Success Story:
Chance Meeting Leads to Opportunity

As Argi had previously participated in a Field School in China, she was able to greet the executives in Mandarin. She delivered her part of the presentation very well and at the end she connected with the program manager and shared details about her current co-op work term working at the non-profit, United Way. Argi and I did not know it at the time, but the program manager was planning on posting a coordinator role that required similar skill sets that Argi had just demonstrated.

This volunteer opportunity she had agreed to participate in turned out to be extremely fortunate for Argi! When the coordinator role was posted, Argi applied for it. She interviewed, was offered the job, and accepted. Since then, she's been promoted to program manager, the role of the person that hired her.

Consider how you can create chances and describe the activities that you will pursue in the table in Step 4.

Step 4: Creating Chances for Happenstance

Activity	Date	Completed

Summary

Building your network *while you are studying* provides you with connections that can help you to realize your meaningful career.

Start building your network by considering who you already know, such as your family and friends. Grow your network by connecting to your instructors, alumni, and industry professionals that come on campus. Consider attending association events keeping in mind the networking tips mentioned. By putting yourself out there, you will invariably find you make your own luck through the concept of planned happenstance!

In the next chapter, "Build Your Profile", I will share with you some tips on how to build your **digital profile**.

Checklist

Build your Network:

Add to your Informational Interview Contact Plan

- ☐ Family
- ☐ Friends
- ☐ Family of your friends
- ☐ Instructors
- ☐ Guest speakers
- ☐ Alumni
- ☐ Industry professionals
- ☐ Potential mentors

Identify three industry associations

- ☐ Sign up for the newsletter
- ☐ Join as a Student Member
- ☐ Attend an event in-person or virtually
- ☐ Volunteer

Outline your plan for planned happenstance

- ☐ Take a class directly or remotely connected to an interest of yours
- ☐ Contact potential employers to conduct Informational Interviews
- ☐ Network at industry events
- ☐ Volunteer, intern, or apply for a co-op job
- ☐ Talk to the person next to you on the bus
- ☐ Add additional ideas!

CHAPTER 8

Build Your Profile

N ow that you have been building your experience and your network while you are studying, it is key to build a profile so that people can find you.

The benefit of having built your network with industry professionals is you will receive information on new developments. However, you also want to be "found" by employers searching to hire someone with your skills, knowledge, and experience.

In this chapter, the focus is on building your digital profile. Let's begin with the need for a LinkedIn profile.

LinkedIn Profile

LinkedIn is an online social media platform where you post a shortened version of your resume, creating a digital profile. This online profile includes your accomplishments, career history, and links to any school, work or volunteer projects that you have completed. Most importantly, the platform allows you to connect to professionals.

Why would you want to be a member of LinkedIn? According to their website as of May 2021, there are 756 million members from over 200 countries and territories, and over 18+ million members in Canada.[100] According to Omnicore, 40 million members are students or recent graduates.[101]

It is important to have a profile on LinkedIn as members are the exact people you want to connect to. Of those millions of members, 90 million are senior level influencers and 63 million are in decision-making positions.[102] There are also 90,000 schools that have a profile on LinkedIn. Reviewing a school's connections on LinkedIn is a great way to see where alumni end up working. Remember, the alumni network for your school provides you with connections to build your network.[103] When it comes to finding a job, more than 90% of recruiters use LinkedIn regularly and there are over 30 million companies online with millions of job openings posted.[104]

Setting Up Your Profile

When it comes to producing your LinkedIn profile, remember to include a professional headshot as it has been shown to generate 14 times more profile views.[105] Also, include links to your projects and details on your volunteer roles. Make sure to keep your profile up-to-date. Look for opportunities to build your LinkedIn connections while you are studying. Reach out to your classmates, and as previously stated, make an effort to reach out to the people you meet at events using the personalized LinkedIn invite feature. When you send a personalized invite, refer to your original meeting to remind the person who you are, when and where you met, and ask them if they would like to connect on LinkedIn.

A cool feature of LinkedIn is the "Find Nearby" feature. When you are at an event, if you and someone, or even a group of people, all agree to connect, there is no need to exchange business cards. Quickly bring out your phone, open the LinkedIn app and go to My Network. Select the "Find Nearby" feature, and your profile and their profiles will appear, and you can all immediately connect.

Social Media Profiles

Your social media accounts are a great way to profile your accomplishments and your interests. Many employers will review your social media accounts. You can take advantage of social media to highlight aspects of yourself and to share relevant experience. This is an opportunity to show employers your digital communication skills through your posts, showing what you are good at and what you love.

Consider setting up a secondary Instagram account to highlight your baking interests, or wellness tips, or your photography skills. Creating a blog is a great way to demonstrate to potential employers that you have slick design and content creation talents. This is something Sara did and it led to a great opportunity.

**Sara's Success Story:
Show Your Talents 24/7**

Sara, a marketing student, has an Instagram profile and a blog "Vancity Girl" with content that highlighted her creativity and social media skills. When a guest speaker from a social media agency visited her class, she asked the speaker for an Informational Interview. When a position came available at the firm, she applied and was interviewed. It was her Instagram and her blog that put her on the top of the resume pile and why she was offered the position.

Digital Portfolios

myBlueprint

Many high schools in Canada use the online platform developed by myBlueprint, an edtech company that creates digital portfolio and career/life planning software for students in kindergarten to grade 12 and post-secondary.

The myBlueprint web apps are licensed by over 6000 schools in 360+ school boards.[106] Within myBlueprint, you can plan towards high school graduation, complete assessments to uncover your personality type, interests, knowledge, and motivations, or explore post-secondary programs and occupations.

You can also build your own digital portfolio to document your work and demonstrate learning. You can add journal entries, files, photos, videos and audio recordings, organize your posts, and share your digital portfolio with a teacher, post-secondary institution, or potential employer as a presentation of your work samples.[107]

Slideroom

Some employers and universities might require you to submit a digital portfolio as part of an application process. This might be required for a graphic design program where you can profile samples of your work. Slideroom is one platform that many art schools use to evaluate applicants. The school sets up a Slideroom account that can accept the prospective student's images, audio, video, and interactive media.[108]

e-Portfolio

At the University of British Columbia, arts students are encouraged to create an e-Portfolio to capture and showcase assignments that they are proud of to share with employers. Some sample e-Portfolios can be found at www.ubcarts.ca.[109]

Behance

Another platform to consider if you have creative work to showcase is Behance which is part of Adobe. Creative people can showcase their work in the form of profiles comprised of their projects.[110]

Summary

Building your online profile requires you to decide how you want to present yourself. This includes deciding which accomplishments, contributions, and skills you wish to share. LinkedIn is a key platform and allows you to post a profile and host all your connections in one place.

Other places to specifically highlight your digital skills are through your social media accounts, writing your own blog, or by building a digital portfolio. Platforms to showcase projects include myBlueprint, Slideroom, or Behance.

Ensure you take these online opportunities to profile your accomplishments. They are great ways to demonstrate to employers that you have the practical skills and the digital knowledge that they are looking for.

Checklist

☐ Set up a LinkedIn profile

☐ Set up social media accounts that can showcase your interests, skills, and abilities

☐ Consider writing a blog

☐ Develop your own digital portfolio to highlight and showcase your abilities

BUILD

The Build Phase is an exciting one. While you are enrolled in training, you are soaking up new theories and acquiring new knowledge. So, focussing on your studies is key. However, this is only part of your education. Employers will be looking for grads that have learned both the theory and the practical skills they are looking for. Therefore, it is key to look out for opportunities to build your practical skills and experience *while you are studying*.

Build Your Experience

As covered in chapter six, you can build your experience by participating in applied learning activities such as:
- Co-op work terms, internships, and practicums
- Volunteering with clubs or societies on campus or start your own
- Starting a new side hustle to build new skills

- Seeking out volunteer opportunities on campus
- International Field Schools and/or studying abroad to build your intercultural competencies

Build Your Network

In chapter seven, we covered tactics for building your network *while you are studying*. Being connected to employers before you graduate allows you to begin your job search while still in school. Your network will provide you with support, references, and information on jobs posted or in the hidden job market. You can build your network by connecting to those that you already know such as your family, friends, and family of your friends! Other people that you can connect to are your instructors, guest speakers, alumni, and mentors. Through research, you can identify industry associations for connecting to professionals already working in the field. You can join these associations as a student member, volunteer, attend an event, or just sign up for their newsletter. And remember, be open to generating opportunities for chance occurrences!

Build Your Profile

Building your digital profile was covered in chapter eight. This includes setting up a LinkedIn profile and being intentional in how you showcase your interests, skills, and abilities via your social media accounts. There are a variety of platforms that allow you to profile your projects and credentials such as myBlueprint, Slideroom, and Behance.

Next, we will cover the Launch Phase. In these following chapters, there are tips and tricks for you as you apply for the job, get the interview, get the offer, and then start your first day!

PHASE 3
LAUNCH

CHAPTER 9

Apply for the Job

You have come so far! You have moved through Phase 1: Discover: reflecting on what you love, what you are good at, what the world needs, and what you can be paid for— all captured on your *ikigai* diagram. This information has led you to determine what additional education you might require for the careers you would like to explore. Next, you researched which schools and programs to apply to. You determined which schools are of interest and completed the application requirements. Once you received your acceptances, you needed to evaluate, based on your own criteria, which school to enroll in.

You have moved through Phase 2: Build, while at your chosen school: you have focussed on acquiring the skills and knowledge required for the careers that you wish to explore. This learning has provided you with ongoing information to update, add, or adapt your *ikigai* diagram. You have also been busy building your experience, network and profile while you were studying. You have acquired both the theoretical knowledge and the practical skills that employers look for.

Now you are about to graduate and are ready to move to Phase 3: Launch. In this phase you'll learn how to navigate job applications, get the interview, secure an offer, and begin your first day on the job!

Where Do You Find Job Postings?

First things first, where can you find information on available jobs?

Online Listings

There are a lot of jobs to apply for and one of the first places to start searching for them is online. Indeed is rated as the Best Overall Job Search Site and Monster is the Runner-Up, Best Overall Job Search Site according to Balance Careers, list of *Best Job Search Websites of 2021*.[111] At these sites, you can post your resume and set up alerts customized for the type of jobs you are interested in based on the key words you select, sending job postings straight to your inbox.

At Indeed.com you can sign up for alerts using job titles, key words, names of organizations, and locations. According to the website, the most popular searches are for accountants, data analysts, developers, and sales associates.[112] You can also set up alerts with LinkedIn and with government websites such as Work BC. One more place for students and recent grads to find meaningful jobs is at www.talentegg.ca.

A new development in the works is a pilot program called "TikTok Resume" where users can search and apply for job listings posted on TikTok. Twenty companies such as Chipolte,

Sweetgreen, Boston Scientific, Shopify and the NBA, are allowing users to apply for job listings with short videos showcasing their qualifications. [113]

Consider including non-profit organizations in your job search. Charity Village (charityvillage.com) sends out job alerts on behalf of charities and non-profits. You can enter keywords like "marketing" or "event planning" and job postings with those keywords will be emailed to you.[114]

The Hidden Job Market

As discussed previously, you want to also access the hidden job market. The hidden job market contains roles that are not posted but are filled through employers reaching out to their network of contacts. Or the job may be posted, with some candidates hearing about the opportunity directly from their industry connections. To become a part of these inner circles, you need to focus on building your own circle of contacts. When you attend an event and follow up with an executive you have met, then you are building your network. When you arrange to meet someone for an Informational Interview, you are building your network. When you connect with a guest speaker that comes to campus, you are building your network.

If you can share the type of jobs you are looking for with your network and those you meet, you will increase the chances of connecting to opportunities. This happened to Kristi when she attended an industry networking event. Kristi shared that she was interested in a certain field of marketing, which led to her hearing about a job opportunity that she wasn't aware of.

Kristi's Success Story:
Put Yourself Out There

One year, I was taking my class on a field trip to hear a marketing executive speak at an industry association luncheon. I asked my students if anyone wanted to volunteer to introduce the speaker at the event. The student was required to research the speaker, write a brief introduction, and deliver it at a hotel ballroom full of 200 marketing professionals.

Kristi volunteered and delivered a very stirring introduction, knocking it out of the park!

As she left the podium, one of the board members of the marketing association asked Kristi what area of marketing she was interested in. She shared she was very interested in market research. The board member told her that, coincidentally, there was a spot open at the table sponsored by a local market research firm. She was placed there and to her great surprise, found out they were currently looking to hire a co-op student. She followed up, applied, and was offered the co-op work term position.

Kristi is still working in the market research field today!

The Resume

You will require a resume to send to companies or to post online that highlights your accomplishments and skills. There are templates in Microsoft Office that can get you started on resume and cover letter formats. Here are some instructions to find resume templates:

- Open Word.
- On the **File** menu, select **New from Template**.

- In the search box, type "resume" or "cover letter".
- Double-click the template you wish to use.

The key elements to include in your resume are:
- Your contact information
- Summarized information on your experience
- Your education details
- Your work experience
- Your volunteer experience
- List of awards

Master Resume Versus Targetted Resume

One approach is to develop a master resume that includes all your past roles and responsibilities in one master document. You can pull information from your master resume to create a shorter, targetted resume for each role you apply to. To create a targetted resume, you would review your master resume and decide which information to include or exclude for the specific role you are applying for.

You might develop a few targetted versions of your resume, for example, one resume to submit for an event marketing coordinator role and another version of your resume to submit for a social media coordinator role. While this might sound like a lot of work, it is really beneficial. It is considered a best practice to customize your resume, crafting your statements to highlight how your accomplishments match the requirements of the job you are applying for, improving your chances of moving to the interview stage.

Remember, it is often not the hiring manager that sees your resume first but the human resources staff. It is their role to ensure that a candidate's skills and background closely match the requirements outlined in the job description in order for a candidate to proceed to the next stage. Look at it this way, the purpose of your cover letter and your resume is to get you access to the interview.

Chronological Versus Skills-Based Resume

You may have heard about two types of resume formats: chronological and skills-based. According to Prepped, a division of RBC Ventures Inc., and a digital career platform for grads and job seekers, there are a couple of things to consider to help you decide on the right format for you.

You probably know about the chronological format, where you list the roles you have performed in order of when you had those positions. If you have some professional experience related to the role you are applying for and a specific skill set to promote, then a chronological resume might be best. However, if you don't have a lot of professional experience or if you have frequently changed jobs, then a skills-based resume might highlight your capabilities best.[115]

You can find free resume templates at www.fullyprepped.com for either type of resume, chronological or skills-based, in a variety of styles such as modern, creative, or professional. First set up a free account, go to **Resources** and select a resume template. You start by just typing directly into your chosen template.[116]

Here are two sample resumes from www.fullyprepped.com. The professional chronological resume and the skills-based creative resume.[117]

Professional Chronological Resume

YOUR NAME

555-555-5555   email@myemail.com   1 Street, City   Linkedin.com/in/name

PROFESSIONAL SUMMARY

Add a summary of your most important capabilities, skills and experiences. While being truthful and authentic about yourself, make sure you also consider the job you're applying for and what the hiring manager is looking for. Consider leveraging the 'Know Your Strengths' and 'Elevator Pitch' exercises in Prepped to get you started with this section.

WORK EXPERIENCE

Enter Job Position Title Here
Company, Month YYYY - Present

- Add one sentence descriptions of main job accomplishments or accountabilities – we suggest no more than 5 per role.
- In each, highlight 1-2 relevant skills/capabilities you used to achieve those accomplishments and what the result or impact was. Try to ensure a number/frequency in most statements and quantify the impact wherever possible.
- E.g. As an experienced sales manager, I motivated a diverse team through positive reinforcement and ongoing communication/feedback to increase our quarter over quarter sales results by 150%.
- E.g. As an effective communicator, I developed and delivered monthly strategy presentations, aligning over 20 national teams to our annual goals.
- E.g. As a server, I delivered exceptional customer experiences and was consistently rated 9/10 by customers who filled in our restaurant survey.

Enter Job Position Title Here
Company, Month YYYY – Month YYYY

- Continue to add your relevant roles – you don't have to place your entire career history, just the most relevant/recent experiences.

Enter Job Position Title Here
Company, Month YYYY – Month YYYY

- Continue to add your relevant roles – you don't have to place your entire career history, just the most relevant/recent experiences.

Enter Job Position Title Here
Company, Month YYYY – Month YYYY

- Continue to add your relevant roles – you don't have to place your entire career history, just the most relevant/recent experiences.

YOUR NAME

555-555-5555   email@myemail.com   1 Street, City   Linkedin.com/in/name

WORK EXPERIENCE (CONTINUED)

Enter Job Position Title Here
Company, Month YYYY – Month YYYY
- Continue to add your relevant roles – you don't have to place your entire career history, just the most relevant/recent experiences.

EDUCATION

Enter Degree/Diploma Here (e.g. BA) in (Subject)
University, City, Province, Month YYYY – Month YYYY
Any additional details, e.g. Dean's List, Scholarship Awards

Enter Degree/Diploma Here (e.g. BA) in (Subject)
University, City, Province, Month YYYY – Month YYYY
Any additional details, e.g. Dean's List, Scholarship Awards

Enter Degree/Diploma Here (e.g. BA) in (Subject)
University, City, Province, Month YYYY – Month YYYY
Any additional details, e.g. Dean's List, Scholarship Awards

PROFESSIONAL SKILLS

Communication
Data Insights
Building Relationships
Critical Thinking
Innovation

AWARDS OR CERTIFICATIONS

Award Name
Organization, City, Province
Month YYYY
Any additional details

Certification Name
Organization, City, Province
Month YYYY

TECHNICAL SKILLS

Microsoft Office
Adobe Creative Suite
HTML
Jira
InVision

LANGUAGES & OTHER INTERESTS

Add as pertinent or delete – this is a valuable place to add any community or volunteer work.

Source: https://www.fullyprepped.ca/en/resources/templates/worksheets–and–tip–sheets/resume–type, accessed Sept 27th, 2020.

Skills-based Creative Resume

YOUR NAME

CONTACT INFO

📞 555-555-5555

✉ email@myemail.com

📍 1 Street, City

in Linkedin.com/in/name

OBJECTIVE

Description of desired area of work and your unique strength as a candidate; option to add industry/role if relevant; e.g. Ambitious professional with a knack for team building and driving results looking to apply my skills as a project manager in the Healthcare industry.

EDUCATION

Enter Degree/Diploma Here (e.g. BA) in (Subject)
University, City, Province
Month YYYY – Month YYYY
Any additional details, e.g. Dean's List, Scholarship Awards

Enter Degree/Diploma Here (e.g. BA) in (Subject)
University, City, Province
Month YYYY – Month YYYY
Any additional details, e.g. Dean's List,

SUMMARY OF QUALIFICATIONS

- Summarize most relevant roles/experience in paid or unpaid work (include number of years); e.g. 5 years of experience working and volunteering in hospitals and retirement living facilities.
- Most relevant degree, training or certification for this role; e.g. Effective project manager with a PMI certification.
- Summarize your most relevant accomplishment/skill/attributes; e.g. Able to plan, coordinate, and monitor tasks and projects from conception to completion.

SKILL HIGHLIGHTS

Skill/Capability Name
- Include unique actions and outcomes beginning with action verb, leveraged from paid or unpaid work/academic or life experience.
- We recommend leveraging our 'Unexpected Strengths' exercise if you do not have relevant professional experience.

E.g. Networking and Partnering
- Led the Silent Auction committee for a local charity fundraiser. Effectively leveraged the networks of the board and managed these relationships to compile over 20 items for the auction, raising $5500.

E.g. Business Communication
- Created and presented a social media strategy to a large corporation as part of my university coursework - received positive feedback from the executives, and several of the recommendations have been implemented.

EXPERIENCE HISTORY

Most Recent Title
Organization, City, Province
Month YYYY - Month YYYY

E.g. Volunteer - Programs
Silver Ridge Seniors Centre, City, Province
Month YYYY – Month YYYY

E.g. Server
Big Eats Restaurant, City, Province
Month YYYY – Month YYYY

YOUR NAME

TECHNICAL SKILLS

Microsoft Office
Adobe Creative Suite
HTML
Jira
InVision

SKILL HIGHLIGHTS (CONTINUED)

Skill/Capability Name

- Include unique actions and outcomes beginning with action verb, leveraged from paid or unpaid work/academic or life experience.
- We recommend leveraging our 'Unexpected Strengths' exercise if you do not have relevant professional experience.

Skill/Capability Name

- Include unique actions and outcomes beginning with action verb, leveraged from paid or unpaid work/academic or life experience.
- We recommend leveraging our 'Unexpected Strengths' exercise if you do not have relevant professional experience.

LANGUAGES & OTHER INTERESTS

Add as pertinent or delete – this is a valuable place to add any community or volunteer work.

AWARDS

Award Name
Organization, City, Province
Month YYYY
Any additional details

Award Name
Organization, City, Province
Month YYYY
Any additional details

Award Name
Organization, City, Province
Month YYYY
Any additional details

CERTIFICATIONS

Certification Name
Organization, City, Province
Month YYYY

Certification Name
Organization, City, Province
Month YYYY

Source: https://www.fullyprepped.ca/en/resources/templates/worksheets-and-tip-sheets/resume-type, accessed Sept 27th, 2020.

Developing Your Resume

Contact Information

Let us start with the first category of information you want to include on your resume: your contact information.

Include your name, address, phone number, email address, and add any additional links to digital properties you own such as your own website, blog, or digital portfolio. You might add your LinkedIn URL if you wish.

Objective/Summary of Skills

Some resume formats include a paragraph at the top called either "Objective" or "Summary of Skills". Including an Objective section allows you to show how your experience connects to the job you are applying to. It is important for the reader to quickly see how the role you are applying for fits with your career progression so far.

Here is an example of an Objective statement:

Objective

I am seeking a marketing coordinator role to build upon my experience in event planning and graphic design.

If you prefer, you can have a section titled "Summary of Skills" instead. Here you succinctly summarize your background for the reader. Add in some descriptive words about your strengths and work style and place this section right at the top of your resume.

Here is an example of a Summary of Skills statement:

Summary of Skills

I am a dedicated, strong communicator with digital marketing experience gained while working on social media campaigns for my university's student marketing club.

Education

The next section to appear in most resume formats is Education. Here you list the type of credentials earned (certificate, diploma, or degree), the dates completed, and the name of the school(s) you attended. If you are currently completing your credentials, you can include the date you started the program and the expected date of completion.

Here is an example of how to set up the Education section:

Education
Business Management Diploma, Langara College
Sept 2021 expected completion April 2023

Work Experience

Next, is the Work Experience section. For each of your previous and current roles, outline the following: job title, company name, the date when you started to the date you finished the role.

Include the key responsibilities and accomplishments for each role. I would suggest bullet points as they clearly and concisely convey this information compared to writing out your accomplishments in paragraph format.

For this section, you want to show what you uniquely bring to any role that you take on. For example, do you improve efficiency? Achieve sales targets? Responsibly manage budgets so effectively that you do not overspend? Include numerical data to support the impact you made—it will really enhance this section.

Here is a sample Work Experience statement:

Work Experience
Western Canada Sales Rep
XYZ Company, Vancouver BC   May 2019 - May 2020

- Managed a territory to increase sales by 20% versus the previous year same time
- Worked closely with the Western Canadian sales force of 20 representatives implementing processes to reduce delivery times by 2 days
- Successfully delivered profit and sales targets for territory of $50,000 during May 2019 – May 2020

Volunteer Experience

Next is the section called "Volunteer Experience". For this section, include relevant volunteer roles that show you have some related experience, even if it is unpaid. Include club leadership participation and any volunteer projects.

A sample of the Volunteer Experience section here:

Volunteer Experience
Director of Sponsorship for the Digital Marketing Club working with a team of volunteers to successfully raise $4,000 in cash and in-kind donations over one year.

Awards

Included in the next section, the "Awards" section, list scholarships or honours you have received and any recognition you have been awarded. Don't be modest! Here's an example:

Awards
Awarded the Trevor Jones Scholarship for highest mark achieved in digital marketing course, 2019

According to an INC article, Google Senior Vice President, Laszlo Bock, has some additional tips. Consider these tips from someone that has reviewed over 20,000 resumes!

- Focus on impact
- Include data and examples

- A clean and consistent format
- Ensure relevance to the job description
- Be fearless—don't be afraid to brag![118]

The Cover Letter

Some employers will request a cover letter with your resume. The goal of the cover letter is to highlight for the hiring manager how your experiences match the criteria in the job description. In addition, it is important to include why you would like to work for the company and what skills and contributions you would bring—refer to your *ikigai* diagram!

The typical order of a cover letter is to begin with a sentence that outlines the title of the role you are applying for and where you saw the role advertised. For instance, did you find it on their website or posted on LinkedIn?

Next, I would recommend including a positive statement about the organization you are applying to. You could refer to the great service that the company provides or commend the innovative products that the firm produces. Refer to something that you genuinely admire about the organization.

Review the job description closely and highlight how you match the criteria they are seeking. For example, if the organization is looking for a positive, friendly person to work in a customer service role, then make sure to mention that you are a positive, outgoing person that enjoys interacting with people. You could refer to previous customer service-type interactions you have had with people. Ensure that you identify other requirements from the job description that you meet.

Last, include the unique strengths that you would bring to the role. State that your resume is attached and that you are available, at their convenience, to meet in person or virtually.

Job Hunting is a Job

Treat job hunting as a job in itself. Keep yourself on track by preparing a job-hunting to-do list each day. Make a list of organizations in the field you will research. Set a target number of calls and emails that you will complete per day. Aim to set up two or three coffee chats, virtual meetings, or Informational Interviews per week. This will keep you focussed and you will be busy learning about the industry and companies that you are interested in, allowing you to update your *ikigai* diagram.

Maintain an exploration mindset. It's a two-way street. Yes, you are looking for an employer to offer you a job but you also want to set yourself up for success and find the right opportunity for you, too. Use the information that you have discovered about yourself that is captured in your *ikigai* diagram as a gauge or guide. It is a touchstone to help you evaluate roles that you are applying to. The questions you want to ask yourself are: "Does this role allow me to do what I am good at, do what I love, and be fairly compensated?" And, "Does this role align with my values, allowing me to be in a meaningful career?"

The Waiting Game

Once you have applied for a position, you will need to wait on the company's response. It is a time of uncertainty because the final outcome is unknown. Therefore, it is key to stay positive. You will secure an opportunity! Try to see this as a chance to find the best place to bring your skills and talents.

Staying Positive

Schedule time for exercise. It will relieve stress and take your mind off job searching for a period of time. Other strategies include adding in a meditation practice to allow your mind to not "do" anything for part of the day. This will allow you to reset and perhaps receive some inspiration. Make sure to get enough sleep, it is important and benefits the brain. It is suggested that seven or eight hours is needed for adults and that sleep improves your longevity, manages your appetite, and helps your immune system and your memory![119]

Managing Stress Tips:

- Engage in yoga or meditation
- Chat with a friend on the phone
- Wander in nature
- Relax with a good book
- Go for a run or jog
- Reframe stress to see it as a challenge or opportunity
- Play with your pet
- Write down five things you are thankful for

These stress reducing tips are from: www.VIAcharacter.org/topic/stress.[120]

Summary

Applying for jobs requires that you know about them! Setting up a profile on job search sites like Monster or Indeed and signing up for their job alerts are ways to find out about opportunities. If you share with your own personal network that you are looking for work, you will have others looking out for you and forwarding you job opportunities. As you build your network, you might receive information on jobs in the hidden job market.

You will need to develop a resume and I have provided some formats and instructions on how to write key sections. When applying for a role, you will include a well-drafted cover letter to capture the attention of the hiring manager. And remember that this process is really a numbers game, meaning you will have to send out many applications in order to secure an interview.

Once you get an interview, you will need to prepare for it, and the next chapter outlines some tips to help you prepare so that you will have a successful experience.

Checklist

☐ Set up profiles and job alerts on job search sites

☐ Share with your network that you are looking for job opportunities

☐ Draft your master and targetted resumes

☐ Use targetted cover letters

☐ Stay positive!

CHAPTER 10

Get the Interview

If you have applied for a role and the organization has contacted you for an interview, then take a moment to congratulate yourself. You have successfully made it to the next stage! However, many people get anxious or stressed when they are asked to be available for an interview. This is quite normal. Remember, too, that the hiring process can take time. If you want to start work immediately after graduation, start the process before then. However, if you reframe it in your mind and see the hiring process as an opportunity for both you and the company to determine if you are a fit, this might relieve some of the pressure you feel.

Consider the interview as a two-way street. While the company is interviewing you to determine if you are a fit, you are also determining if the organization is a fit for you. You're evaluating the organization's culture, values, and work styles. Remember to check in with your *ikigai* diagram and use it as a reference.

So how do you prepare for an interview?

Interview Preparation

Pre-Prep

Prior to your interview, try to arrange a coffee chat or virtual meeting with someone that currently works or has worked at the organization. Once arranged, you can ask them questions about the company culture, what they like about the company, and what they would change about the company if they could. You should know that the hiring manager expects that you have researched their organization. They are interested in finding out why you want to work there. If it appears you are just going through the motions and that you just want to find any job, that is not very appealing to them.

Employers are interested in candidates that demonstrate they have investigated the organization and can share reasons why they really want to work there. Be prepared to share these reasons. Be authentic. Just think of what you like and admire about the firm. Is it the organization's position on the environment? Or perhaps you feel their products and services are innovative and offer customers great solutions. Is there something you can identify about the organization that just feels right? Or perhaps there is something about the company's values that aligns with your inner *ikigai* touchstone.

Next, let's prepare what to say at the interview.

Three Key Points About You

When preparing for an interview, consider identifying three key points about yourself that you want to convey during the interview. This will ensure that you are focussed on sharing the key contributions that you would bring to the role. Write these points down and have them with you during the interview so that before you leave, you can consult your notes to ensure you have shared them.

Key points to include? The unique strengths and skills that you bring. Or perhaps you want to make sure that before you leave the interview, you have shared how your previous work or volunteer experience has prepared you. Think of these three key points as the ways you differ from the other candidates.

Step 1: Three Key Messages to Convey in an Interview

1. _____

2. _____

3. _____

Often, the first question you will be asked is to tell them a little bit about yourself. It is best to draft something that is succinct. Refer to your elevator pitch as a starting point. If you are still in school, you might include what program you are in, what year you are in, and when you will be graduating. Also, briefly give a summary of your work and volunteer experience. Keep this introduction very short as the additional interview questions they will ask will allow you to expand on your work and volunteer experience.

Additional questions to expect and prepare for:

- What are your strengths and weaknesses?

- What would you consider your greatest achievement?

- Why are you interested in this role and company?

Many firms use a form of questions called behavioural-based questions. The assumption is that when you share how you behaved in a past situation, describing how you handled that event, the interviewer gets a sense of how you might handle a similar situation in the future. It is recommended that you prepare ahead of time. Try to have two or three past situations that you can refer to when answering these types of questions.

Here are some behavioural-based questions aimed at uncovering your organizational ability.

> Q. Share a time when you were working on a project. What did you do to ensure that you met your targets? What did you put in place to monitor your progress?

Or here is a three-part question that aims to uncover information about your interpersonal skills.

> Q. Tell me about a time when you had to work with a difficult person. What made this experience difficult? How did you resolve the situation with this person?

Behavioural-Based Questions and the STAR Approach

There is also a trick to answering the behavioural-based questions called the STAR approach.

STAR stands for: Situation, Task, Action, Result.[121] You begin telling the story by briefly describing the Situation and outlining the Task or what you had to do. Next, you describe the Actions you could have taken and which one you decided to take, and then outline the Result.

The key is not getting too involved in the story, especially if it was a difficult situation. You want to get in and out, providing the interviewer with an example that demonstrates you handled the situation successfully.

Step 2: Answering Behavioural-Based Questions

Here are six common questions to prepare for:

1. Describe a time when you faced difficulties completing your goal. How did you move around them?

    _____

    _____

    _____

    _____

2. Describe a time when your supervisors or co-workers gave you feedback about your work or actions. What did you learn about yourself?

    _____

    _____

    _____

    _____

3. Tell me about a time when you successfully handled a change or shift in priorities.

    _____

    _____

    _____

    _____

4. Describe a time when you had to understand a different point of view to solve a problem.

_____

_____

_____

_____

5. Tell me about a time when you had co-workers with different ideas all working on a project. What did you do to pull them together?

_____

_____

_____

_____

6. Tell me about a time when you had a complicated problem to solve. Outline the problem and describe how you approached it.

_____

_____

_____

_____

Salary

Salary may or may not be brought up by the interviewer. However, be prepared and determine your target salary ahead of time. Arm yourself with salary information you have gathered online—both job search websites Monster.ca and Indeed.com also offer salary tools.

If the interviewer asks you what salary you have in mind, ask them to share with you the role's salary range first. Once you know the salary range, you can then determine if your target salary is within their range or not. Then reflect on the level of experience you bring to this role and be prepared to explain how your experience justifies where you might be placed within that range. Your experience, plus knowing your market value, may make it possible to demonstrate that you should be placed on the middle or higher end of the range.

Have Questions for the Interviewer

It is quite common for the interviewer to ask you at the end of the interview if you have any questions for them. As previously stated, this is an opportunity to further explore if the organization is a fit for you and aligns with your *ikigai* findings.

Come prepared with a few questions. The questions can be about the role or about the company/work environment. You can incorporate any knowledge that you have gained from coffee chats or Informational Interviews that you have had with current or former employees of the organization.

Here are some fantastic questions to ask employers from a blog article written by Prepped. As previously mentioned, when you visit this platform you will find many fun, informative activities, articles, resume and cover letter templates, and other tools for job search. Just go to www.fullyprepped.ca for more information.[122]

Questions about the role:

1. How would you describe the ideal candidate?

2. Can you tell me more about the day-to-day responsibilities of the role?

3. Can you describe a typical work day, or week, for this job?

4. What is the typical career path for someone in this role?

5. What immediate projects or tasks would I be working on?

6. How does this role help your department achieve its goals?

7. What are the major metrics for the person in this position?

8. What are you hoping the successful hire will achieve in the first three months?

9. What are the major goals for this role in the coming year?

Questions about the company/work environment:

1. Can you tell me more about the leadership team for this group?

2. What are the biggest opportunities or threats facing the company right now?

3. What do you like best about your job/working for this company?

4. What is the organization's management style?

5. How does the team work/interact?

6. What do employees enjoy the most about working here?

7. What has your career been like at this organization?

8. What are some of the highlights?[123]

Step 3: Select Three Questions to Ask the Employer During The Interview

1. _____

_____

2. _____

_____

3. _____

_____

Closing of the Interview

At the closing of the interview, be prepared to ask if the interviewer has any doubts. They may not, but it is worth seeing what you can uncover. Consider asking if there is anything about your background or experience that they may have hesitations about. This allows you to hear a concern they may have and gives you the opportunity to address it before you leave the interview. Cassie had this happen in an interview for her dream job.

Cassie's Success Story:
Closing the Deal

Cassie had just graduated from animation design. At the end of her interview, she asked the interviewers if they had any reservations. They were concerned about her lack of experience. Cassie was able to reassure them, stating that she was a fast learner and one who is comfortable seeking out answers on her own. We are not sure if that was the key to alleviating all their fears but she was offered the job the next day!

Before you leave the interview, have one last look at your notes to ensure you mentioned the three key points you had planned on conveying, then ensure that you thank the interviewer(s). Ask what the timeline is for the hiring process and what the next steps are. When you leave, make sure to clearly state you are really interested in the role. Remember, the goal of the interview is to get an offer, and then you can reflect on whether to take the offer or not.

Providing Your References

At a certain point in the hiring process, you may be asked to provide your references. Some companies request references when you apply or they request your references only when you are being seriously considered for the role. Your references are key and it is highly recommended that you both inform your references they will be contacted and that you prepare them for the call. Typically, three references are requested. Consider bringing your list of references to the interview on a separate page. Ensure the layout of the reference page matches the look and feel of your cover letter and resume.

How do you choose someone to be a reference? You should select someone that has seen your work habits. This might be a teacher, volunteer supervisor, manager, or co-op work term manager. Try not to select a reference who is a close family member or a friend unless they were also your supervisor and have seen you in a work environment or volunteering capacity.

You need to ask the people you have in mind for permission to list them as a reference. Once they have agreed, ask them their preferred way to be reached. For instance, would they prefer to be reached by email or would they prefer the employer call their cell phone? When preparing your list of references, ask your references what they would say about you so you know you are selecting references that will be complimentary.

It is a thoughtful practice to let your references know ahead of time that you are interviewing for a role and that you might be providing their information to the company. When you ask someone to be a reference for you, it is helpful if you send them the job description you applied to. In addition, consider providing your references with a brief paragraph of why you think you are a good fit for the role. You may wish to highlight something specific, such as information you failed to mention in your interview, so that your references can speak to it if asked by the interviewer.

Reflect on who you can use as a reference and capture their name and contact information in the table in Step 4.

Step 4: Name of Three References and their Preferred Contact Information

Name	Preferred Contact Information

The Interview Day: Remote or In-Person?

Of course, whether you are meeting in-person or online, ensure you have showered and dressed up for the interview, as first impressions do count. Here are three tips for setting up your interview for success.

Tip #1 Choose a Good Location if it's a Remote Interview

If you are meeting over Zoom or a video conference platform, select a location for the interview where you will be undisturbed. Test the connectivity and lighting to evaluate how you appear on screen. Be aware of the room you will be interviewing in as this background will appear to your interviewer. Make sure it is tidy or consider using a virtual background, choosing one that looks professional. Notify roommates you are not to be interrupted and keep pets out of the room you will be using.

Tip #2 Arrive Early For An In-Person Meeting

If you are meeting in person, it is a good habit to arrive early. Travelling somewhere for the first time can be stressful, so plan your route in advance and leave extra time to get there, in case transit runs late or finding a parking spot proves tough. Arriving early means having a few minutes to take some breaths and approach the interview in a calm state.

When you arrive, you might need to check in with the receptionist and let them know your name, who you are meeting, and at what time your appointment is. The receptionist will then contact the person and then typically someone comes to meet you to take you to the room with the interviewer(s).

Tip #3 Smiles and Handshakes

Give a nice smile and firm handshake when you meet the interviewer(s). When you sit down, it is appropriate to have a notebook with notes, including the three key messages you want to convey and your prepared questions for the interviewer. Bring your resume and perhaps your references list. Take a deep breath and try to enjoy the interview.

It is quite likely that you apply for a role but do not get an offer. However, recognize that interviewing with key players can lead to opportunities later that you might not see in the moment! This happened to Andrew and Dean.

Andrew's and Dean's Success Story: On the Sidelines is OK

Andrew and Dean saw that their college's Co-op and Career Centre posted an entry-level marketing role at the foundation of Vancouver's professional football club, the Whitecaps. This was a dream role for both of them, they both applied and were interviewed. Neither received an offer. However, they were both offered volunteer positions as Ball Managers. They attended all home matches and supervised the Ball Kids around the pitch. A fantastic opportunity to do what they love!

This connection to the Whitecaps allowed them to connect with players on the team and when Andrew and Dean developed a soccer program for children in Africa, one of the players donated items. Travelling to Africa, Andrew and Dean provided balls, uniforms, and equipment to the children. Andrew and Dean's connections to the Whitecaps and the experience they gained developing their soccer program helped them secure full-time dream jobs with the club! Andrew was hired in sales and Dean was hired in marketing.

Source: Dean Tsatouhas. Dean Tsatouhas and Andrew Kocicka Volunteering, 2013, photograph, Kenya

Moral of the story? You never know what can happen when you put yourself out there!

Summary

In this chapter, we covered tips and tricks for a successful interview. That includes preparing three key messages that you wish to leave with the hiring manager, practicing answering behavioural-based questions using the STAR response technique, and preparing two or three past situations that you can easily recall and share. Interview preparation also includes writing down questions you will ask the interviewer at the end of the session. And last, you should arrange to have three references that can speak about you. You will need to share their contact information with the interviewer.

On the day of the interview if remote, select a good background. If in-person, arrive early and make sure to give a nice smile and firm handshake.

If the interview goes well and you are a fit, then you will receive an offer! In the next chapter, "Get the Offer", you'll find out how to evaluate and negotiate the offer.

Checklist

☐ Prepare your three key messages to convey to the interviewer

☐ Review the behaviour-based questions

☐ Rehearse recalling several past situations using the STAR response technique

☐ Prepare your questions for the interviewer

☐ Prepare your list of three references

CHAPTER 11

Get the Offer

Waiting for the offer may take some time and this waiting can be painful! The organization will send you the offer once they have all the paperwork and approvals complete. You might receive a phone call, followed by a written offer, and an agreement to sign and return to them.

Negotiation

Salary

Before you sign, you might have an opportunity to negotiate the salary. However, before you negotiate the salary you should have a sense of what you are worth. Your career centre might have information on salary ranges for entry level careers in your field. Or government websites such as www.workbc.ca have salary ranges for a variety of careers. Or as mentioned previously, look up the salary tools at www.Monster.ca and www.Indeed.com.

Your offer may reflect your discussions in the interview if salary was brought up at that time.

If you know the salary range of the role, determine if you can negotiate how your experience will allow you to "hit the ground running", justifying a higher placement in the range. Consider mentioning the value you will bring based on what money you saved at your previous company or how you increased sales.[124]

Other Benefits

Review the offer for its vacation details. Consider negotiating for additional paid vacation days and/or additional unpaid vacation days, if having time off is important to you. Ensure you are clear on if the company is an all 'in office' workplace or has a hybrid in-person/work-from-home model.

Make sure to understand the company's benefits package. Also review it for annual allocated professional development or training funds. If not, this might be something to negotiate. You only get what you negotiate for, so take some time to see if you can improve the offer at this stage, prior to accepting.

Should you Accept?

When evaluating whether to accept an offer or not, refer to your *ikigai* diagram to help you to decide. Does the role allow you to do what you love and what you are good at? Is it a role that is well paid? Does the role allow you to work with an organization that is aligned with your values and is addressing the world's problems?

Your *ikigai* diagram is a way to evaluate if the role would be a good step on your meaningful career journey. Once you receive the final offer, read it over carefully to ensure what you had agreed upon is included. Sign it and send it back. Share your great news with your references!

Summary

Getting an offer is very exciting! Be sure to review the offer, looking at all the details. You may be able to negotiate the salary and other benefits. Knowing what the typical role is worth is helpful information allowing you to negotiate a fair offer for yourself.

Evaluate against your *ikigai* diagram and check in with yourself as you decide if this role supports your meaningful career path.

Checklist

- ☐ Review the details of the offer, salary and other benefits
- ☐ Negotiate if possible
- ☐ Check in with your *ikigai* diagram
- ☐ Sign the offer
- ☐ Let your references know you got the job!

CHAPTER 12

First Day on the Job

Congratulations! This is a great accomplishment. You are moving along your meaningful career journey.

And relax! It is very natural to feel nervous or excited on your first day. Realize that you may feel deskilled or feel as if you have lost all the skills you came with. This is because you are temporarily in an environment where you must learn the basics—for instance, how to communicate with your team and when and where people meet for lunch.

Most organizations provide training through an onboarding process. With onboarding, typically someone is assigned to show you around and provide you with your computer, login identification numbers, keys, entry codes, etc.

You may be introduced to quite a few people during your first week. When you meet someone, try to remember their name! There are memory tricks to help you remember a person's name such as repeating it back to them, right after you hear it. For example, "Great to meet you, **Carla**." Another trick is to make a mental note and connect their name to some information about them for instance Carla works in the Customer Care Department.

Congratulations on beginning your meaningful career journey! I want to wish you all the very best success with your new job! You have done an amazing amount of work moving through the three Phases: Discover, Build, and Launch. While this is a milestone to celebrate, it is also the beginning of the next chapter in your adventure! I don't want you to feel you are on your own now that you have started your career. Please recognize that all the work and skills you have developed throughout this book are life-long skills. You can and should revisit the three Phases of Discover, Build and Launch, over and over as you continue on your journey.

LAUNCH

We covered in the Launch Phase: how to apply for the job, prepare and be successful at the interview, get the offer, and, finally, covered some tips for the first day on the job.

Apply for the Job

This chapter covered how to find out about jobs through setting up alerts and connecting to others that know about the hidden job market. Tips on preparing your resume and your cover letters were also covered in this chapter.

Get the Interview

Successful interviews come from preparation. Thinking ahead about the three key messages that you wish to leave with the hiring manager and practicing behavioural-based question answering using the STAR response technique will have you feeling confident. Interviewers expect that you will have questions for them, so come prepared to ask the interviewer either about the role or the company. If the interview goes well and you are a fit, then you may receive an offer!

Get the Offer

It is very exciting to receive an offer. Use your *ikigai* diagram to guide you in your analysis of the role and the company as you check in with yourself to decide if this role is a good step along your meaningful career journey. If so, we discussed how to review the offer and look for opportunities to negotiate salary and other benefits. Based on research you have conducted, an understanding of what the role might be worth will empower you to negotiate a fair offer for yourself.

First Day on the Job

While exciting, you may find you feel unsettled and tired at the end of your first day. Expect this and be kind to yourself recognizing that this is only temporary.

In the next section, the Conclusion, we'll reflect on how you can revisit the three phases: Discover, Build, and Launch as you move along your meaningful career journey. You can continue to check in with and modify your *ikigai* diagram using it as a guide or touchstone.

CONCLUSION

Re-Discover, Re-Build, Re-Launch

encourage you to use this exploration mindset throughout your whole life. As you move along your career journey, continue revisiting your *ikigai* diagram and its four circles to check if you are still feeling on-purpose. Use the *ikigai* diagram as a touchstone to check-in with yourself. Your career journey is dynamic and as time passes, you might adjust or pivot.

For instance, after some time in a role, you will grow and change. Sometimes the organization changes or the economy changes. Keep checking in with yourself to see if you are still doing what you love. Does your role continue to allow you to do what you are good at? If yes, then that is great!

However, there may come a time when you find that the role isn't allowing you to use your strengths or do what you are good at, or what you love. This will be important information to recognize. At this point, you may need to approach your manager to see if there are creative ways to find some additional duties where you can contribute your skills. Or you might discover that you have grown and would benefit from moving to another role at the same organization.

As you progress in your career, be alert to see if the values of the organization you work for still align with your values. Reflect and keep confirming if the environment allows you to do meaningful work. Over time, the company might change—or you might change—and this might mean looking for new opportunities at another organization.

You will also want to keep up-to-date with trends and reports that outline the skills employers look for. Keeping up with labour market information and forecasts of skills in demand will allow you to anticipate and prepare yourself as the world changes. You might see an opportunity to enroll in additional training, ensuring you have the most in-demand, up-to-date skills.

On your career journey, you will continue to discover more about yourself, the job market, and how the world needs you.

Phase 1: Discover and Re-Discover

During your career, continue to revisit the diagram and its four circles to check if you are still feeling on purpose. The *ikigai* diagram is like a guide that changes. Update, add or adapt it as you explore and learn new things about yourself and the world.

Phase 2: Build and Re-Build

I am sure you have guessed it! Yes, you will need to continue to build your skills, experience, and network, updating your profile as you progress during your career. Learning is a lifelong activity and as you see the job market change or as you develop and seek out new opportunities, you will be building new skills and experiences. In addition, as you grow in your career, you will continue to build your network. Your resume and online profile are works-in-progress and are the best places to capture your accomplishments, courses taken, certifications received, and any new skills learned.

Phase 3: Launch and Re-Launch

Once launched into your first job, there will come a time after you have outgrown that role—when you might consider a "re-launch". This happens when you feel that the role is no longer allowing you to fulfill your *ikigai*.

Sometimes a re-launch is forced on you—perhaps when a pandemic hits, for instance—or when the job market shifts, resulting in the need for you to learn some new skills. Perhaps you will need to re-launch yourself into another career. By working through the steps in this book, you have the tools and techniques to determine your next stop on your journey.

Last Words

The work that you have done to know yourself and to embrace an exploration mindset are life-long tools supporting you as you navigate your career. By continuing to check in with your *ikigai* diagram, you ensure that you will be doing what you love, what you are good at, you're tackling what the world needs, and getting paid to do it.

Best of luck on your meaningful career journey. Keep in touch, and share your successes with me at:

Stephanie@BackpacktoBriefcase.ca.

Acknowledgements

The writing of this book has been a fantastic experience. While it has had its ups and downs, I have been amazed by the support I have received along the way.

I would like to acknowledge that I live, work, and wrote this book while situated on the traditional, unceded, and occupied ancestral lands of the Musqueam, Squamish and Tsleil-Waututh Peoples.

I wish to acknowledge the wonderful people that have provided their input, feedback, and permission to include their stories and so graciously encouraged me through the process.

Thank you to my business partner and Co-Founder of Peer-Spectives Consulting, Louann McCurdy, for her ongoing guidance and feedback. You have been a great sounding board!

Thank you to my book coach Suzanne Doyle-Ingram for her guidance and tough love! Thank you to the first people to read the manuscript, Christian Westin, Heather Workman, and Alison Grbic for your encouraging comments and insights. Thank you to Susie Poulsen, Patty Aroca-Ouellette, Joyce Wong, Carolyn Wing, and Melissa Breker as you were some of the first people to show interest in the workshops, coaching, and digital camps offered by PeerSpectives Consulting.

For their ongoing support throughout the writing of the book, I would like to thank Linda Purcell, Anne DeWolfe, Francie Deveau, Lynn Kitchen, and many others who have been so supportive through the process.

Thank you to Brigette Liang for your attention to detail in preparing the citations and to Angie Ishak for the editing and wonderful layout of the book! Thank you to Connie Reichelsdorfer for your digital support. And a special shout out to my daughter Kayli Koonar for her graphic design skills in preparing some of the images included in the book.

I would like to thank the many students that I have had the privilege to teach—you have provided me with such an enriched life. Thank you to those students that provided their permission for including their success stories in the book.

Thank you to the e2grow team for their support in the development of an accompanying online course for this book, specifically Dr. Peter Baloh.

I wish to thank my dearest sister Alison for her constant and unstoppable love and support. I would like to thank my mother Audrey, and my dad Trevor and his wife Susan for their suggestions and interest in the development of the book.

And last, my success in writing this book is due to the tireless support from my loving and patient husband, Kevin, and from my wonderful children, Kayli and Kyle! Thanks for being such great cheerleaders!

About the Author

Stephanie Koonar, MBA, BA Psychology, is a marketing professional, academic, career coach and team-building facilitator. She is a community connector with strong marketing and business development experience, at the international, national and regional levels in a variety of sectors such as telecommunications, wine and spirits, market research, experiential marketing, non-profit marketing, and post-secondary education (teaching and administration). She has experience working with international teams that were based in Dublin, Milan, Guadalajara and London.

Stephanie teaches marketing management courses to undergraduate and post-degree college students, having taught over 4,000 students. With a focus on supporting students as they transition to the workplace, she is involved in many initiatives that help students build their experience and build their network. As the former Assistant Chair, External Relations for the Langara School of Management, she was responsible for strengthening partnerships with community organizations, businesses and leading industry associations to increase opportunities for students and connect to the community. Stephanie is the Greater Vancouver Board of Trade Mentor-of-the-Year, 2018 and the Teaching Excellence Award winner, 2018.

Stephanie has developed and taught many courses and programs and was most recently part of a multi-university team researching ways to support employers to attract, hire, and onboard students from international pathways. She has championed the building of intercultural competencies for all students while in the role of Intercultural Engagement Consultant.

As Co-Founder of PeerSpectives Consulting Company, Stephanie and her business partner empower purpose-driven individuals and organizations to be their best through facilitating team-building workshops and one-on-one coaching programs. Stephanie is a Gallup-Certified Strengths Coach.

As a child, Stephanie emigrated from England to Canada, grew up in Ontario and now enjoys living and working in beautiful Vancouver, British Columbia, with her husband and two young adult children.

Connect with Stephanie Koonar on LinkedIn or email her at Stephanie@BackpacktoBriefcase.ca.

References

1. Nicolas Boyon, "The State of Happiness in a COVID World," Ipsos, October 7, 2020, https://www.ipsos.com/en/global-happiness-study-2020.

2. Margaret Rouse, "Ikigai," TechTarget, April 2016, https://whatis.techtarget.com/definition/ikigai.

3. Work BC, "WorkBC's Career Trek," Province of British Columbia, accessed January 15, 2020, www.careertrekbc.ca.

4. Xello, "How it works". Xello, accessed Jun 12, 2021, https://xello.world/en/middle-and-high-school-ca/

5. Lillian Cunningham, "Myers-Briggs: Does it Pay to Know Your Type?", Washington Post, December 14, 2012, https://www.washingtonpost.com/national/on-leadership/myers-briggs-does-it-pay-to-know-your-type/2012/12/14/eaed51ae-3fcc-11e2-bca3-aadc9b7e29c5_story.html.

6. "Do What You Are: Discover the Perfect Career for You Through the Secrets of Personality Type by Paul D. Tieger, Barbara Barron, and Kelly Tieger," Amazon Canada, accessed December 30, 2019, https://www.amazon.ca/Do-What-You-Are-Personality/dp/031623673X.

7. 16 Personalities, "Core Theory: Our Framework," NERIS Analytics Ltd., accessed February 4, 2020, https://www.16personalities.com/articles/our-theory.

8. Jim Clifton and Jim Harter, It's the Manager: Gallup Finds That the Quality of Managers and Team Leaders is the Single Biggest Factor in Your Organization's Long-Term Success, (New York: Gallup Press, 2006), 2.

9.   Tom Matson and Jennifer Robison, "Using a Strengths-Based Approach to Retain College Students", Gallup, April 5, 2018, https://www.gallup.com/workplace/236063/using-strengths-based-approach-retain-college-students.aspx

10.   Donald O. Clifton, Edward "Chip" Anderson and Laurie A. Schreiner, StrengthsQuest: Discover and Develop Your Strengths in Academics, Career and Beyond, (New York: Gallup Press, 2006), 4.

11.   Mary Reckmeyer, Strengths Based Parenting: Developing Your Children's Innate Talents, (New York: Gallup Press 2016), 25.

12.   Donald O. Clifton, Edward "Chip" Anderson and Laurie A. Schreiner, StrengthsQuest: Discover and Develop Your Strengths in Academics, Career and Beyond, (New York: Gallup Press, 2006), 2.

13.   Karlanne Gomez, Tiffany Mawhinney and Kimberly Betts, "Welcome to Generation Z," Deloitte: Network of Executive Women, accessed February 19, 2020, https://www2.deloitte.com/content/dam/Deloitte/us/Documents/consumer-business/welcome-to-gen-z.pdf

14.   iid, "Step Aside Millennials: Gen Z Has Arrived," Medium, March 18, 2020, https://blog.prototypr.io/step-aside-millennials-gen-z-has-arrived-161f48499c49.

15.   Roger L. Martin and Sally Osberg, "Social Entrepreneurship: The Case for Definition," Stanford Social Innovation Review, Spring 2007, https://ssir.org/articles/entry/social_entrepreneurship_the_case_for_definition.

16.   Xerez Haffenden, "Social Enterprises are on the Rise in Canada," ShareVision Blog, July 2, 2014, https://www.sharevision.ca/blog/social-enterprises-are-on-the-rise-in-canada.

17.   "Langara Grad Implements Social Enterprise Expansion That Started as a School Project," The Abbotsford News, November 18, 2019, https://www.abbynews.com/marketplace/langara-grad-implements-social-enterprise-expansion-that-started-as-a-school-project/.

18.   Tim Clydesdale, The Purposeful Graduate: Why Colleges Must Talk to Students about Vocation, (Chicago: University of Chicago Press, 2015), 122.

19.   Shawn Achor, The Happiness Advantage: The Seven Principles of Positive Psychology That Fuel Success and Performance at Work, (New York: Crown House, 2010), 78.

20.   "The Weekly STAT," Brainstorm Strategy Group, accessed January 17, 2021, https://www.brainstorm.ca/weekly-STAT.

21.   "About Us", SheEO, accessed January 17, 2021, https://sheeo.world/about-us/.

22.   "Sustainable Foundations: A Guide for Teaching the Sustainable Development Goals," Manitoba Council for International Cooperation," Feb 2018, page iii accessed Jan 31st, 2021.

23. "Ignite the Future," SparkPath, accessed September 27, 2020, https://mysparkpath. com/pages/about.

24. "Hasta la Raíz: Down to the Root," Patagonia, accessed October 10, 2020, https:// www.patagonia.ca/home/.

25. Simon Sinek, Start with Why: How Great Leaders Inspire Everyone to Take Action, (New York: Penguin Books, 2011).

26. "Industry Overview: Nonprofits," University of British Columbia, last updated April 27, 2017, https://sba.ubc.ca/blog/industry-overview-nonprofits.

27. "Contact the Choose Love Team," Choose Love, accessed January 21, 2020, https:// choose.love/pages/contact-us.

28. "Introducing the 2021 Canadian Nonprofit Sector Salary and Benefits Report", page 9, accessed May 18, 2021 https://charityvillage.com/introducing-the-2021-canadian-nonprofit-sector-salary-benefits-report/

29. Certified B Corporation, "About B Corps." B Lab, accessed January 5, 2021, https:// bcorporation.net/about-b-corps.

30. Certified B Corporation, "About B Corps." B Lab, accessed May 18th, 2021 https:// bcorporation.net/faqs.

31. Gary T. Reker, "The Meaning of Life," in The World Book of Happiness, ed. Leo Bormans, (Richmond Hill: Firefly Books, 2011), 136.

32. Province of British Columbia, British Columbia Labour Market Outlook: 2019 Edition Report, 2019, https://www.workbc.ca/Labour-Market-Industry/Labour-Market-Outlook.aspx.

33. Province of British Columbia, British Columbia Labour Market Outlook: 2019 Edition Report, 2019, 19, https://www.workbc.ca/Labour-Market-Industry/Labour-Market-Outlook.aspx.

34. "Fourth Industrial Revolution," World Economic Forum, accessed February 14, 2021, https://www.weforum.org/focus/fourth-industrial-revolution.

35. "Preparing Tomorrow's Workforce for the Fourth Industrial Revolution: For Business: A Framework for Action," Deloitte Global and Global Business Coalition for Education, September 2018, https://www2.deloitte.com/content/dam/Deloitte/global/Documents/About-Deloitte/gx-preparing-tomorrow-workforce-for-4IR. pdf.

36. RBC, Bridging the Gap: What Canadians Told Us About the Skills Revolution Report, May 2019, 2, https://www.rbc.com/dms/enterprise/futurelaunch/_assets-custom/pdf/RBC-19-002-SolutionsWanted-04172019-Digital.pdf.

37. RBC, Bridging the Gap: What Canadians Told Us About the Skills Revolution Report, May 2019, 2, https://www.rbc.com/dms/enterprise/futurelaunch/_assets-custom/pdf/RBC-19-002-SolutionsWanted-04172019-Digital.pdf.

38. RBC, The Coming Skills Revolution: Humans Wanted: How Canadian Youth Can Thrive in the Age of Disruption Report, March 2018, 16, https://www.rbc.com/dms/enterprise/futurelaunch/_assets-custom/pdf/RBC-Future-Skills-Report-FINAL-Singles.pdf.

39. This page includes information from the https://www.onetcenter.org/tools.html O*NET Career Exploration Tools by the U.S. Department of Labor, Employment and Training Administration (USDOL/ETA). Used under the https://creativecommons.org/licenses/by-nd/4.0/ CC BY-ND 4.0 license. O*NET® is a trademark of USDOL/ETA.

40. This page includes information from the https://www.onetcenter.org/tools.html O*NET Career Exploration Tools by the U.S. Department of Labor, Employment and Training Administration (USDOL/ETA). Used under the https://creativecommons.org/licenses/by-nd/4.0/ CC BY-ND 4.0 license. O*NET® is a trademark of USDOL/ETA.

41. "ITA-Educators-Pack-Ed-3.zip", ITA Youth, 5, accessed Dec 26th, 2020, https://youth.itabc.ca/educators/overview/.

42. "Arborist Technician," ITA Youth, accessed December 22, 2020, https://youth.itabc.ca/trade/arborist-technician/.

43. "Horticulturist, Landscape," ITA Youth, accessed December 22, 2020, https://youth.itabc.ca/trade/horticulturist-landscape/.

44. "Crane Operator," ITA Youth, accessed December 22, 2020, https://youth.itabc.ca/trade/crane-operator/.

45. "Heavy Equipment Operator," ITA Youth, accessed December 22, 2020, https://youth.itabc.ca/trade/heavy-duty-equipment-operator/.

46. "Baker," ITA Youth, accessed December 22, 2020, https://youth.itabc.ca/trade/baker/.

47. Province of British Columbia, British Columbia Labour Market Outlook: 2019 Edition Report, 2019, https://www.workbc.ca/Labour-Market-Industry/Labour-Market-Outlook.aspx.

48. "Instrumentation Control Technician," ITA Youth, accessed December 20, 2020, https://youth.itabc.ca/trade/instrumentation-control-technician/.

49. "Trades A-Z: Explore Trades," ITA Youth, accessed December 20, 2020, https://youth.itabc.ca/trades-a-z/.

50. "The Builder: Raise the Roof on Your Career," ITA Youth, accessed May 3, 2021, https://youth.itabc.ca/trade-type/builder/.

51. "Trades A-Z: Explore Trades," ITA Youth, accessed November 15, 2020, https://youth.itabc.ca/trades-a-z/.

52. "Aircraft Maintenance Technician," ITA Youth, accessed November 15, 2020, https://youth.itabc.ca/trade/aircraft-maintenance-technician/.

53. "ITA-Educators-Pack-Ed-3.zip" http://youth.itabc.ca/educators/overview ITA_Youth_Educators_Presentation_Deck_web-1.pdf page 17, accessed Dec 26th, 2020

54. Work BC, "Explore Careers," Province of British Columbia, accessed February 19, 2020, https://www.workbc.ca/Jobs-Careers/Explore-Careers.aspx.

55. Province of British Columbia, British Columbia Labour Market Outlook: 2019 Edition Report, 2019, https://www.workbc.ca/Labour-Market-Industry/Labour-Market-Outlook.aspx.

56. "Does Education Pay? A Comparison of Earnings by Level of Education in Canada and its Provinces and Territories", Statistics Canada, last modified April 3, 2019, https://www12.statcan.gc.ca/census-recensement/2016/as-sa/98-200-x/2016024/98-200-x2016024-eng.cfm?wbdisable=true#n4.

57. "Does Education Pay? A Comparison of Earnings by Level of Education in Canada and its Provinces and Territories", Statistics Canada, last modified April 3, 2019, https://www12.statcan.gc.ca/census-recensement/2016/as-sa/98-200-x/2016024/98-200-x2016024-eng.cfm?wbdisable=true#n4.

58. Marc Frenette and Kristyn Frank, Economic Insights: Earnings of Postsecondary Graduates by Detailed Field of Study Report, Statistics Canada, last modified March 11, 2016, https://www150.statcan.gc.ca/n1/pub/11-626-x/11-626-x2016056-eng.htm

59. Maxine Betteridge-Moes, "Top Ten Most Valuable Degrees in Canada," RBC, January 13, 2020, https://discover.rbcroyalbank.com/top-ten-most-valuable-degrees-in-canada/.

60. Will Nott, "Half of Learners in Top Study Destinations Say HE Fails to Prepare for Career," The Pie News, November 27, 2019, https://thepienews.com/news/almost-half-of-learners-in-top-destinations-say-higher-ed-failed-to-prepare-them-for-their-career-survey/.

61. Will Nott, "Half of Learners in Top Study Destinations Say HE Fails to Prepare for Career," The Pie News, November 27, 2019, https://thepienews.com/news/almost-half-of-learners-in-top-destinations-say-higher-ed-failed-to-prepare-them-for-their-career-survey/.

62. Gina Shereda, "Backward Design Your Way to a Fulfilling Career," Inside Higher Ed, November 11, 2019, https://www.insidehighered.com/advice/2019/11/11/benefits-starting-end-mind-you-pursue-your-career-opinion.

63. Work BC, "Explore Careers," Province of British Columbia, accessed February 19, 2020, https://www.workbc.ca/Jobs-Careers/Explore-Careers.aspx.

64. "About SchoolFinder.com.", School Finder, accessed December 28, 2020, https://www.schoolfinder.com/About/Site.aspx.

65.   "How It Works," Study in Canada, accessed December 28, 2020, https://www.studyincanada.com/MyAccount/MyAccount.aspx.

66.   "Your Ultimate Guide to Choosing a University," QS Top Universities, accessed December 29, 2020, https://qs.topuniversities.com/grad/apply/your-ultimate-guide-to-choosing-a-university.

67.   The World University Rankings, "World University Rankings 2021," Times Higher Education, accessed January 17, 2021, https://www.timeshighereducation.com/world-university-rankings/2021/world-ranking

68.   University of Victoria, email message to Kyle Koonar, January 10, 2020.

69.   Diego Fanara of Unibuddy, email message to Stephanie Koonar, October 28, 2020.

70.   "Our Story: Connecting Peers for Better Decisions," UniBuddy, accessed October 18, 2020, https://unibuddy.com/about/.

71.   "Chat with a Current Domestic U of G Student," University of Guelph, accessed October 18, 2020, https://admission.uoguelph.ca/chat-with-domestic-student.

72.   "Your Ultimate Guide to Choosing a University," QS Top Universities, accessed December 29, 2020, https://qs.topuniversities.com/grad/apply/your-ultimate-guide-to-choosing-a-university.

73.   "The Grade 11 Success Formula: What to Do in Grade 11 to CRUSH IT in Grade 12!," MyCampus GPS, accessed August 6, 2020, www.mycampusgps.ca.

74.   "About ScholarshipsCanada.com.", ScholarshipsCanada, accessed December 28, 2020, https://www.scholarshipscanada.com/About/Site.aspx.

75.   "Canada Student Grants and Loans – What Student Grants and Loans Offer," Government of Canada, modified April 28, 2020, https://www.canada.ca/en/services/benefits/education/student-aid/grants-loans.html.

76.   "RESP Rules and Contribution Limits," RBC Royal Bank of Canada, accessed August 23, 2020, https://www.rbcroyalbank.com/investments/resp-rules-contribution-limits.html.

77.   "Loyalty Programs: HigherEdPoints Loyalty Program Participants," Higher Ed Points Inc., accessed September 20, 2020, https://www.higheredpoints.com/loyalty-programs/.

78.   "Participating Institutions," HigherEdPoints, accessed September 20, 2020, https://www.higheredpoints.com/participating-institutions/.

79.   "Student Budget Worksheet," Government of Canada, December 12, 2019, https://www.canada.ca/en/financial-consumer-agency/services/budget-student-life/student-budget-worksheet.html.

80. "Calculate Your Budget," Coast Capital Savings Federal Credit Union, accessed December 27, 2020, https://apply.coastcapitalsavings.com/budget/?_ga=2.207333651.1883526440.1609106229-1734838599.1596570860.

81. "What is WIL?", Association for Co-Operative Education and Work-Integrated Learning BC/Yukon, accessed March 22, 2021, https://acewilbc.ca/what-is-wil/.

82. RBC, Bridging the Gap: What Canadians Told Us About the Skills Revolution Report, May 2019, 2, https://www.rbc.com/dms/enterprise/futurelaunch/_assets-custom/pdf/RBC-19-002-SolutionsWanted-04172019-Digital.pdf.

83. RBC, Bridging the Gap: What Canadians Told Us About the Skills Revolution Report, May 2019, 2, https://www.rbc.com/dms/enterprise/futurelaunch/_assets-custom/pdf/RBC-19-002-SolutionsWanted-04172019-Digital.pdf.

84. "Preparing Tomorrow's Workforce for the Fourth Industrial Revolution: For Business: A Framework for Action," Deloitte Global and Global Business Coalition for Education, September 2018, 16, https://www2.deloitte.com/content/dam/Deloitte/global/Documents/About-Deloitte/gx-preparing-tomorrow-workforce-for-4IR.pdf.

85. RBC, Bridging the Gap: What Canadians Told Us About the Skills Revolution Report, May 2019, 2, https://www.rbc.com/dms/enterprise/futurelaunch/_assets-custom/pdf/RBC-19-002-SolutionsWanted-04172019-Digital.pdf.

86. Hart Research Associates, Falling Short? College Learning and Career Success: Selected Findings from Online Surveys of Employers and College Students Conducted on Behalf of the Association of American Colleges & Universities, January 20, 2015, 4, https://www.aacu.org/sites/default/files/files/LEAP/2015employerstudentsurvey.pdf.

87. "Youth Interns," Coast Capital Savings Federal Credit Union, accessed November 2, 2020, https://www.coastcapitalsavings.com/about-us/our-community/programs-for-youth/youth-team.

88. "Preparing Tomorrow's Workforce for the Fourth Industrial Revolution: For Business: A Framework for Action," Deloitte Global and Global Business Coalition for Education, September 2018, 41, https://www2.deloitte.com/content/dam/Deloitte/global/Documents/Atout-Deloitte/gx-preparing-tomorrow-workforce-for-4IR.pdf.

89. "Your Voice, Your Future – Wave 4 Results: What Students are Thinking in the Coronvirus Crisis," School Finder Group, accessed January 5, 2021, https://schoolfindergroup.com/wave-4-what-students-are-thinking-in-these-difficult-times/.

90. "Identify Your Purpose. Accelerate Your Growth," Apologue, accessed May 28, 2020, https://apologue.net.

91. "Identify Your Purpose. Accelerate Your Growth," Apologue, accessed May 28, 2020, https://apologue.net.

92. International Education, "Building on Success: International Education Strategy (2019-2024)," Government of Canada, last modified February 3, 2020, https://www.international.gc.ca/education/strategy-2019-2024-strategie.aspx?lang=eng.

93.   Mark S. Granovetter, "The Strength of Weak Ties," American Journal of Sociology 78, no. 6 (May 1973): 1360-1380, https://sociology.stanford.edu/sites/g/files/sbiyb-j9501/f/publications/the_strength_of_weak_ties_and_exch_w-gans.pdf.

94.   Fanshawe College, "Matching Students with Alumni for Inspiring Career Conversations," Ten Thousand Coffees, accessed February 19, 2020, https://www.tenthousandcoffees.com/schools/fanshawec.

95.   Dave Wilkin, "A Piece of Advice for New Grads: Networking Doesn't Have to Be Intimidating," Globe and Mail, last updated November 20, 2019, https://www.theglobeandmail.com/business/careers/career-advice/article-networking-doesnt-have-to-be-intimidating-just-reach-out-and-have-a/.

96.   "Leaders of Tomorrow," Greater Vancouver Board of Trade, accessed February 19, 2020, https://www.boardoftrade.com/programs/leaders-of-tomorrow.

97.   John D. Krumboltz, "The Happenstance Learning Theory," Jounal of Career Assessment 17, no. 2 (May 2009): 135–54, https://doiorg/10.1177/1069072708328861.

98.   John D. Krumboltz, "The Happenstance Learning Theory," Journal of Career Assessment 17, no. 2 (May 2009): 135–54, https://doi org/10.1177/1069072708328861.

99.   Bernard D. Beitman, Connecting with Coincidence: The New Science for Using Synchronicity and Serendipity in Your Life, (Deerfield Beach: Health Communications, Inc., 2016).

100.   "About Us: Statistics," LinkedIn Pressroom, accessed May 5, 2021, https://news.linkedin.com/about-us#Statistics.

101.   Salman Aslam, "LinkedIn by the Numbers: Stats, Demographics & Fun Facts," Omnicore, last updated February 10, 2020, https://www.omnicoreagency.com/linkedin-statistics/

102.   Salman Aslam, "LinkedIn by the Numbers: Stats, Demographics & Fun Facts," Omnicore, last updated February 10, 2020, https://www.omnicoreagency.com/linkedin-statistics/

103.   Salman Aslam, "LinkedIn by the Numbers: Stats, Demographics & Fun Facts," Omnicore, last updated February 10, 2020, https://www.omnicoreagency.com/linkedin-statistics/

104.   Salman Aslam, "LinkedIn by the Numbers: Stats, Demographics & Fun Facts," Omnicore, last updated February 10, 2020, https://www.omnicoreagency.com/linkedin-statistics/

105.   John Nemo, "How to Make Your LinkedIn Profile 20x More Appealing, According to Science," Inc., January 4, 2017, https://www.inc.com/john-nemo/how-to-make-your-linkedin-profile-20x-more-appealing-according-to-science.html.

106.   MyBlueprint, "Empowering Students to Make Informed Decisions About Their Future," Doublethink Inc., accessed November 1, 2020, https://myblueprint.ca/about.

107.   "MyBlueprint, "All About Me Resources," Doublethink Inc., accessed November 1, 2020, https://www.myblueprint.ca/support/resources/all-about-me/2ELFs-BOU7O4GuMw6KwaMgG/.

108.   "Overview," SlideRoom, accessed February 19, 2020, www.slideroom.com.

109. "UBC Arts ePortfolios," University of British Columbia, accessed November 1, 2020, https://ubcarts.ca/ accessed.

110. "Guide: Intro to Behance," Behance, accessed March 24, 2021, https://help.behance.net/hc/en-us/articles/204483894-Guide-Intro-to-Behance.

111. The Balance Careers, "Best Job Search Websites: Find Your Next Dream Gig in No Time," Dotdash, accessed March 25, 2021, https://www.thebalancecareers.com/top-best-job-websites-2064080.

112. "Find Jobs," Indeed, accessed January 15, 2020, www.indeed.com.

113. "Move Over LinkedIn: Chipotle, Shopify And Other Employers Are Flocking to TikTok for Young Talent," accessed May 18th, 2021 https://www.forbes.com

114. "Find Your Position with Purpose," Charity Village, accessed March 10, 2020, www.charityvillage.com.

115. Prepped, "Worksheets and Tip Sheets," RBC Ventures Inc., accessed September 27, 2020, https://www.fullyprepped.ca/en/resources/templates/worksheets-and-tip-sheets/resume-type.

116. Prepped, "Worksheets and Tip Sheets," RBC Ventures Inc., accessed September 27, 2020, https://www.fullyprepped.ca/en/resources/templates/worksheets-and-tip-sheets/resume-type.

117. Prepped, "Worksheets and Tip Sheets," RBC Ventures Inc., accessed September 27, 2020, https://www.fullyprepped.ca/en/resources/templates/worksheets-and-tip-sheets/resume-type.

118. Peter Economy, "Google Career Experts Say That to Get Your Next Job, Your Resume Should Always Have These 5 Simple Things," Inc., January 3, 2020, https://www.inc.com/peter-economy/google-career-experts-say-that-to-get-your-next-job-your-resume-should-always-have-these-5-simple-things.html?cid=search.

119. "How Does Seven to Eight Hours of Sleep Affect Your Body?", Healthline, accessed February 1, 2020, https://www.healthline.com/health/science-sleep-why-you-need-7-8-hours-night.

120. "Topics: Stress," VA Institute on Character, accessed February 19, 2020, https://www.viacharacter.org/topics/stress.

121. Alison Doyle, "How to Use the STAR Interview Response Method," The Balance Careers, March 6, 2020, https://www.thebalancecareers.com/what-is-the-star-interview-response-technique-2061629.

122. Prepped, "Worksheets and Tip Sheets," RBC Ventures Inc., accessed September 9, 2020, https://www.fullyprepped.ca/en/resources/templates/worksheets-and-tip-sheets/resume-type.

123. Prepped, "Questions for Employers," RBC Ventures, accessed May 28, 2020, https://www.fullyprepped.ca/blog/.

124. Kim Lankford, "Step-By-Step Guide to Negotiating a Great Salary," Monster, accessed March 25, 2021, https://www.monster.ca/career-advice/article/Salary-Negotiation-Guide-Canada.

Your *ikigai* Diagram

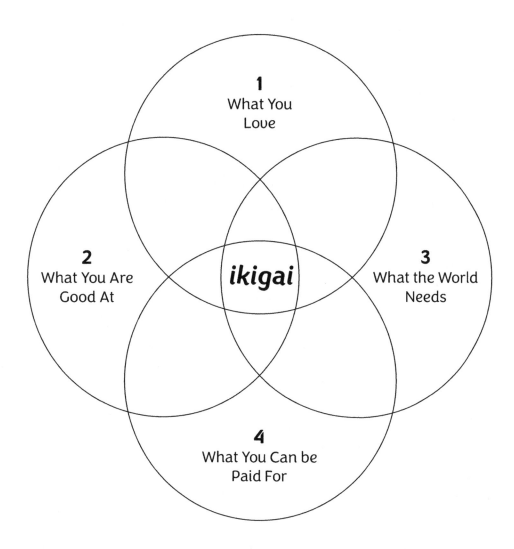

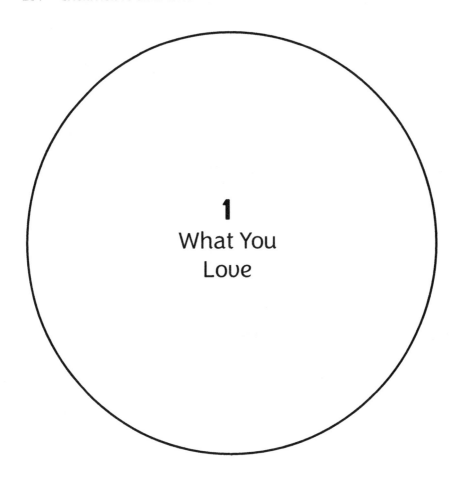

1
What You
Love

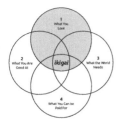

This work is a derivative of Ikigai-EN.svg by Nimbosa, an adaptation from works in the PUBLIC DOMAIN by Dennis Bodor (SVG) and Emmy van Deurzen (JPG), CC BY-SA 4.0 <https://creativecommons.org/licenses/by-sa/4.0>, via Wikimedia Commons/ Some words removed from the original.

2
What You Are
Good At

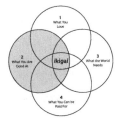

3
What the World Needs

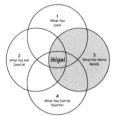

Made in the USA
Middletown, DE
19 August 2021